"In retirement, guaranteed income may be more important than savings because savings can run out due to longevity, stock market risk, and taxes. Mark Mappa shows you strategies that can help you maximize your monthly income with the goal for it to last as long as you do. That's why cash flow is king!"

Ed Slott, CPA, author, retirement expert, founder of www.irahelp.com

"Mark does an incredible job of laying out the simple truth that cash flow is king. Unfortunately, we as investors spend too much time focusing on rates of return and assets but not enough time on income. A successful retirement is dependent on two things: Income (and I would argue increasing income for life) and risk management (taking key retirement risks off the table). A comfortable and independent retirement can be obtained with the use of reliable strategies to provide retirement income. This book can help you down that path."

Tom Hegna, economist, best-selling author, retirement income expert

"Financial freedom is an indispensable part of human freedom. Mark Mappa provides practical guidance on how you can achieve your financial freedom and especially when you will likely need it most—at retirement. This book provides a real-world explanation of terms and concepts of the financial planning tools that are available by using a step-by-step approach to help you to identify and evaluate your choices as well as understanding the potential consequences of your decisions. I encourage you to begin your journey to financial freedom with Mark Mappa!"

Yuri N. Maltsev, PhD
Professor of Economics at Carthage College

"We live in a world of widespread financial ignorance. Mark Mappa has undertaken the task to address a variety of financial topics in his new book. Developing an understanding of these topics will certainly serve the reader well."

Paul A. Cleveland, PhD
Professor of Economics and Finance at Birmingham-Southern College

"*Cash Flow Is King* addresses the all too common misconception that retirement planning ends at retirement. Mark offers sound strategies for generating a reliable and sustainable postretirement income."

Kristen MacKenzie, MBA, CFP®, CRPC®
Professor at the College for Financial Planning

"This book will be a valuable resource to those who are serious about planning for retirement. The information provided is well worth reading and incorporating into your retirement plans."

Ted Benna
401k Benna, LLC

"Mark Mappa has produced an excellent guide to help people and their advisors produce better financial outcomes. In particular, Mappa has created a highly engaging explanation of sequence of returns risk that people can really understand. He taps into issues that can affect all of us; it is definitely worth your time."

Ken Mungan, Chairman, FSA, MAAA,
Milliman Financial Risk Management

"Mark brings to light points that are often overlooked in a concise and articulate manner that make sense. In an often-confusing financial advisory world, Mark helps to simplify things. His insights can be invaluable to anyone, from expert level to novice, who is looking for wealth management advice."

David Cyrs, President, MS, AIF, CFP®, CRC
CYRS Wealth Advisors, LLC

"*Cash Flow Is King* is a real gem! Not only does this book conquer common financial misconceptions, it also provides a badly needed and rigorous roadmap for discerning investors on how to properly tap retirement income. Sadly, many investors have been so entrenched in wealth accumulation mode, they've given almost no thought to intelligent de-accumulation strategies. The good news is this book will provide a solid framework for helping to maximize cash flow right when most people will need it most—during retirement!"

Ron DeLegge, Founder and Chief Portfolio Strategist
ETFguide.com

"*Cash Flow Is King* will help you to think outside the box and apply strategies that can work in real life and that are not just based on unproven theories or hypotheticals. This is a must read."

Jessica Reed, CPA
Reed Accounting

"I usually don't enjoy reading these types of books and most times find them full of jargon and complicated concepts that only financial planner geeks understand. Not the case here. I loved the examples that accompany the financial concepts that Mark lays out. Dispelling the misconceptions is a great way to start the discussion vs. having to search the entire book to get some straight talk out of the way. My favorite chapter is Chapter 3, 'How the Wealthy Save and Invest.' Great discussion and interesting concepts. Overall easy to read and understand. It feels like you are having a one-on-one conversation as you read."

Perry Sholes, President
Kraft Foods Alumni Network

"Mark's book, *Cash Flow Is King*, is must-reading for any investor or retiree looking for common sense ideas on managing their money. More importantly, Mark helps make it easy to understand. As a CPA, I understand the need to seek appropriate tax advantages not just on the path toward retirement but also during retirement. Mark's strategies can help you achieve this objective and help you to not outlive your retirement income in the process."

Jim Hechtman, CPA, Managing Partner
The Hechtman Group, LTD

"The sad reality today is that many people who consider themselves savvy, informed investors are anything but. They follow the latest trend and jump on the next big thing thinking they understand what's going on but may not have a real understanding of the basic economics that drive true wealth accumulation. This lack of understanding can be even more prevalent when it comes to distribution planning. In *Cash Flow Is King*, Mark gives you the foundation and basis to develop the analytical skills necessary to truly become a seasoned, well-informed investor for both your accumulation and distribution phases of life."

Kevin Crown, President
The Association of Financial Educators

CASH FLOW

IS

KING

Mark A. Mappa

MSFS, CFP®, ChFC, CLU, RFC, CFS, CIS, CES

Cash Flow Is King
Copyright © 2019 by Mark A. Mappa

First Edition: 2019

For bulk purchases, special orders, and other inquiries, contact:
Mappa Wealth Management
2700 Patriot Blvd., Suite 250, Glenview, IL 60026
(847) 262-3030
mark@mappawm.com

ISBN (paperback): 978-0-578-48827-1

Produced in the United States of America

Book designer: Ken Kendzy

Publishing consultant: Andrew Chapman, Social Motion Publishing

Dedication

To my wife, Rachel: your love, dedication, and support are unparalleled. My success has a great deal to do with having you in my life. Thank you for all that you do. To my three children: Zackary, Tanner, and Sophie. I wish you all the success and happiness in the world. There is nothing you can't achieve if you put your mind to it. I do what I do for all of you.

This book is also dedicated to each of my clients (and future clients), who have entrusted me with their money. That is an enormous responsibility and I take it extremely seriously. I always have and always will look out for what's in your best interest. Thank you for your trust, confidence, support, and your business.

Disclosures

Nothing contained herein is to be considered a solicitation, research material, an investment recommendation, or advice of any kind. The information contained herein may contain information that is subject to change without notice. Any investments or strategies referenced herein do not consider the investment objectives, financial situation, or needs of any specific person. Product suitability must be independently determined for each individual investor. Woodbury Financial Services and Mappa Wealth Management explicitly disclaim any responsibility for product suitability or suitability determinations related to individual investors.

Some of the investments or products discussed herein are considered complex products. Such products contain unique risks, terms, conditions, and fees specific to each offering. Depending upon the product, risks include, but are not limited to: issuer credit risk, liquidity risk, market risk, and the performance of an underlying derivative financial instrument, formula, or strategy. Return of principal is not guaranteed above FDIC insurance limits and may be subject to the creditworthiness of the issuer.

You should not purchase an investment product until you have read the specific offering documentation and understand the specific investment terms and risks of such investment. Any guarantee of benefits discussed may be subject to the claims-paying ability of the underlying company. Neither asset allocation nor diversification guarantee a profit or protect against a loss in a declining market. They are methods used to help manage investment risk.

All examples provided are hypothetical and are not intended to reflect past or future performance of any specific investment or index. It is not possible to invest directly in an index. Actual results will fluctuate with market conditions and will vary. These examples also ignore the impact of fees, expenses, and taxes, if applicable.

The following were used in some of the calculations to provide examples for this book: the Hewlett-Packard financial calculator, Excel formulas, and financial website calculators. Other calculators or formulas may yield slightly different values resulting in, for example, differences due to frequency of compounding, rounding, etc. However, this doesn't impact the points of the examples being presented.

All charts, graphs, illustrations were reproduced with permission.

Certified Financial Planner Board of Standards Inc. owns the certification marks CFP®, CERTIFIED FINANCIAL PLANNER™, CFP® (with plaque design) and CFP® (with flame design) in the U.S., which it awards to individuals who successfully complete CFP Board's initial and ongoing certification requirements.

Mappa Wealth Management
2700 Patriot Blvd., Suite 250
Glenview, IL 60026
(847) 262-3030
Securities and Investment Advisory Services offered through Woodbury Financial Services Inc., Member FINRA, SIPC, and Registered Investment Advisor. Mappa Wealth Management and Woodbury Financial Services are not affiliated.

Contents

Important Terms and Definitions Discussed in This Book

Please refer to this page as needed when you come across these terms.

Accumulation phase. The period in which you are saving and investing toward a goal, such as retirement; also, referred to as the wealth-building phase.

Asset correlation. A measure of how assets move in relation to one another and when. When assets move in the same direction at the same time (up or down), they are considered to be highly correlated. When one asset tends to move up while another goes down, the two assets are considered to be low- or noncorrelated.

Average rate of return. The simple mathematical average of a series of returns generated over a period of time. It's also referred to as the arithmetic average return.

Big brand-name firms. Large financial services firms with brand-name recognition. Examples: Ameriprise, Fidelity Investments, Northwestern Mutual.

Cash flow. The movement of money—whether it's money in or money out—such as from a checking, savings, or investment account. Cash flow represents the financial lifeblood of every government, business, family, and individual.

Cash value life insurance. Life insurance that provides lifelong protection, and the ability to accumulate cash value on a tax-deferred basis. The policyholder can use the cash value for many purposes such as a source for loans, as a source for cash, for investment opportunities, or to pay policy premiums. It is also referred to as permanent life insurance.

Compounded rate of return. The annual percentage return realized on an investment, which is adjusted for changes in prices due to inflation, volatility, or other external effects. It's also referred to as the geometric average return and is the same as real rate of return.

Discount brokerage firms. Financial services firms that provide online trad-

Cash Flow Is King

ing of securities to customers at a lower cost compared to traditional brokerage firms. They cater to do-it-yourself investors who want to trade securities in the stock market. As a result, discount brokerage firms generally offer little to no financial or investment advice or planning. Examples: Charles Schwab, TD Ameritrade, E*Trade, Fidelity.

Distribution phase. The period in which you start withdrawing from your savings and investments for a particular goal, such as retirement.

Market volatility. The fluctuation of the price or value of stocks in the stock market. Low volatility means a minor fluctuation and high volatility means a greater fluctuation.

Media pundit. A person who offers, often through mass media, his or her opinion or commentary on a subject area. The key word here is *opinion*.

Naysayer. Someone who denies, refuses, opposes, or is skeptical or cynical about something or habitually expresses negative or pessimistic views despite a general feeling that things are favorable, positive, or appropriate.

Opportunity cost. The cost of losing a benefit by taking one action over another, for example, losing the ability to earn interest on money you currently have saved or, losing the ability for growth on money you currently have invested, by liquidating it to make a purchase, such as for a car. By not having a car loan, you won't pay interest to the lender for the loan but you will lose the interest earnings on the savings account or the ability to do something else with the money.

Permanent life insurance. See cash value life insurance.

Proprietary investment or financial product. An investment or financial product that is both developed and exclusively distributed for sale by the same company. For example, an insurance policy from Northwestern Mutual is sold only through a Northwestern Mutual sales agency or the brokerage firm acts as both the investment manager and sole distribution channel to sell the investment or financial product to its customers.

Qualified plan. A type of retirement plan established by an employer for the benefit of the company's employees. Qualified retirement plans give employers a tax break for the contributions they make for their employees. They can also allow employees to defer a portion of their salaries into the plan which lowers the employees' income tax liability by reducing their current taxable income.

Real rate of return. See compounded rate of return.

Sequence of investment returns risk. Your exposure to financial loss due to the timing and order in which your investment returns occur during the distribution phase. For example, low or negative returns early in the distribution phase may result in the eventual depletion of the account or forced reduction of the distribution amount to prevent the account from depleting.

Target date fund. A collective investment scheme, often a mutual fund or a collective trust fund, designed to provide a simple investment solution through a portfolio in which the asset allocation mix becomes more conservative as the target date approaches, such as retirement. Also known as a lifecycle, dynamic-risk, or age-based fund.

Volatility. See market volatility.

Wall Street firms. Large financial-services conglomerates (a.k.a. investment banks) providing advisory, financing, and banking services, as well as sales, market making, and research on a broad array of financial products, including equities, credit, currency, commodities, and their derivatives. Examples of Wall Street firms: Bank of America Merrill Lynch, Morgan Stanley, Wells Fargo, JP Morgan Chase, Citigroup.

Preface

I have been an independent financial advisor and a fiduciary for over 30 years. An independent financial advisor does *not* work for Wall Street or one of the big brand-name or discount brokerage financial services companies. I have learned to realize that these companies simply do not provide true independent or unbiased advice. It has been my experience that they will steer customers to their own proprietary investments or financial products because they are the most financially beneficial for the company. However, and this is key, *they may not be the most beneficial for the customer*. There is also often very little, if any, personalized financial advice provided, with most everyone receiving basically the same cookie-cutter or one-size-fits-all plan. In addition, the advisors who work for these companies, have sales quotas that their sales manager or supervisor requires them to meet each month or quarter. Why would anyone want to receive advice from a financial firm under those circumstances, particularly when it comes to something as important and personalized as their financial well-being? Because, unfortunately, most people don't know any better.

In contrast, independent financial advisors are free to choose from a wide range of financial products, investments, and resources, which allows them to provide their clients with far more objective and personalized advice. In fact, independent financial advisors have no obligation or requirement to recommend any specific financial products or investments, nor do they get pressure from a sales manager to meet sales quotas or sell the *product of the month*. In addition, they are not bound to any one insurance company or any proprietary products. Thus, they can be fair and open-minded, and advise their clients on the most appropriate investments and financial products available. This allows them to work in their clients' best interests.[1] This is exactly how I provide financial advice and how a true fiduciary is supposed to act (you'll read more about being a fiduciary in the next section).

I have also found that most advice regarding saving and investing revolves around putting most or all of your money into the stock market. This includes everything from how and where to invest in the stock market and who are the best money managers to earn the highest returns in the stock market, to who can offer the best investment advice when investing in the stock market. This stems from Wall Street and the big brand-name and discount brokerage firms as well as the countless financial and investment; magazines, newsletters, books, podcasts, blogs, and television and radio shows.

This is supposed to lead us to believe that by investing a great deal of our money in the stock market, we will have the best chance to achieve our financial goals. The truth is that the stock market is not the only or even the best option to help achieve our financial goals. This is very critical to understand. That's because it involves a lot of risk, risk that most people don't comprehend or even realize. That risk is further magnified once you are retired. Yet, most people still invest in the stock market because the supposed "financial experts" say to do so or because "everyone else" is doing it. Of course, these "experts" are the ones who typically benefit the most when others invest their money in the stock market.

The truth is, investing in the stock market is gambling. There are no two ways about it. If you don't know the outcome, it's gambling. And no one can tell you the outcome when it comes to investing in the stock market. Even when the discussion is not about the stock market, it's about the bond market which has its own risks and drawbacks as well.

Before you consider investing in the stock market, make note of the following disclosures from the Securities and Exchange Commission (SEC) website regarding investing:

> *All investments involve some degree of risk. If you plan to buy securities—such as stocks, bonds, mutual funds, or ETFs—it's important that you understand that you could lose some or all of the money you invest.*
>
> *Dividends or interest payments may also change as market conditions change.*
>
> *A fund's past performance is not as important as you might think because past performance does not predict future returns. But past performance can tell you how volatile or stable a fund has been over a period of time. The more volatile the fund, the higher the investment risk.*

Now, heed Warren Buffett's rules on investing:

Rule #1: Never lose money.

Rule #2: Never forget Rule #1.

That being said, it's very important to note that I am not suggesting avoiding the stock market altogether. There is certainly a place for some of your money to be invested in the stock market. I have many clients invested in the stock market and I personally have some of my own money invested in it as well. I am simply suggesting to not be overexposed to it or to rely too much on it to achieve your financial objectives. The truth is, there are other, very appropriate financial products that a true fiduciary will consider and present when providing financial advice and that you should be open to as well.

Along with this ill-advised reliance on the stock market, we have also been led to believe that we need to focus on rates of return. In fact, two questions often asked by investors are "What's my rate of return?" and "What kind of rate of return can I expect?" However, we have no control over rates of return, no one does. Instead, what you should focus on is cash flow. That's because unlike rates of return, cash flow is generally more reliable. It can even be guaranteed. In fact, cash flow can be an integral component of your rate of return. Therefore, your saving and investment decisions should include cash flow strategies, even for a long-term goal like retirement. Once you retire, cash flow strategies should become the main component. That's because you can't spend rate of return. However, you *can* spend cash flow which, if you really think about it, is the purpose for saving and investing for retirement in the first place. Unfortunately, most people often overlook or simply dismiss cash flow.

The good news is that I will show you that there are more prudent ways to save and invest your money without having to risk most or all of it by investing it in the stock or the bond market. As I mentioned, some of your money in the stock market or bond market is fine, but certainly not all or even most of your money.

Regarding your retirement income, I will show you why you can't rely on the traditional advice, strategies, or "rules of thumb," we are often taught. Instead, I will show you more prudent ways to generate income by focusing on cash flow.

Finally, when I meet with clients to discuss their goals for retirement, they all pretty much want the same thing: a reliable "paycheck for life." What they don't want is for their retirement paycheck to be impacted by interest rates or the economy—and certainly not the stock market. A rate of return simply can't provide this as a given outcome (as you will learn in this book). By creating reliable and even guaranteed cash flow rather than just seeking a rate of return, I have helped my clients achieve this goal and I can help you as well.

---

[1] There is no assurance that an independent financial advisor will work in your best interest, just like there is no assurance a doctor, lawyer, CPA, mortgage broker, etc. will work in your best interest. However, many of the conflicts of interest inherent with Wall Street and the big brand-name and discount brokerage firms are removed when working with an independent financial advisor.

Being a Fiduciary

Being a fiduciary is very important to the client-advisor relationship. A fiduciary works in the best interest of the client and not the financial services firm he or she works for. As a fiduciary, this is the only way I have ever conducted business. However, the definition of a fiduciary for much of the financial services industry is advising people to invest most or all their money in the stock or bond markets without consideration of other investments and financial products. According to much of the financial services industry, if a financial advisor doesn't meet this narrow standard that *they* created, they will claim the advisor is not acting as a fiduciary. This is an extremely biased point of view and it's certainly unsubstantiated. The fact is, there are plenty of other investments and financial products not directly tied to the stock market that are just as appropriate and, in many cases, even more appropriate for the client.

In fact, per the Certified Financial Planner Board of Standards, Inc. (CFP Board), which holds financial advisors to the highest ethical standard, there are six steps in the financial planning process (see below). Specifically, Step 4 states *Developing and presenting recommendations and/or alternatives.* The key word is *alternatives.* I believe the true definition of a fiduciary is an advisor who considers all the available options and alternatives to help meet their client's goals and objectives. Every financial advisor must understand and adhere to this if they want to be considered a true fiduciary. Simply ruling out or completely dismissing certain investments or financial products because they don't fit into their personal knowledge base or firm's profit agenda is a disservice to the client and degrades the true meaning of fiduciary.

Six steps to the financial planning process:
1. Establishing and defining the client-planner relationship
2. Gathering client data including goals
3. Analyzing and evaluating the client's current financial status
4. Developing and presenting recommendations and/or alternatives
5. Implementing the recommendations
6. Monitoring the recommendations

Introduction

This book is a compilation of my 30-plus years as an independent financial advisor. It is what I have learned from years of independent research on wealth management and financial planning, as well as listening to and learning from other independent experts in the industry.

My many years of experience as a financial advisor have helped me to realize what works and what doesn't work in wealth management and financial planning, specifically when it comes to real-world situations and circumstances. Far too much financial advice is based on hypotheticals that don't always hold up in real-world situations, especially during periods of extreme market volatility or economic crisis.

This book is also about the independent research regarding saving, investing, risk management, financial products, and retirement planning conducted by many of the PhDs in the academic community. In fact, the more research I did for this book, the more I found that the impartial and objective community of academia (the PhDs in economics, finance, statistics, and mathematics) has already done a great deal of independent research on these topics. The concepts, strategies, and financial products I present in this book are supported by the findings of their research. I use this knowledge to help my clients reach their financial objectives.

I am also open-minded and think outside the box. This is very important, because if there are better or more appropriate ways (i.e., alternatives) to offer financial advice, I want to know about them so I can share them with my clients. My goal is to always do what's most appropriate for my clients.

This book is for those who are open-minded and willing to think outside the box too. It is also for those who prefer to believe in the facts and the math rather than opinions that are often false or misleading. In addition, it is for anyone who is concerned about their existing financial plan or strategy and whether it will be sustainable through challenging stock market and economic conditions. It is definitely for anyone who is skeptical about the financial and investment information and advice they are currently receiving. The good news is that there is a different path you can take. This book will show you that path. It is my hope that you will take the knowledge you gain from this book and use it to position yourself and your family for true financial success.

Keep in mind, this book can't and won't provide you with specific investment or financial advice or recommendations. That's because each of you reading this book has your own unique set of circumstances, objectives, and risk tolerance. However, this book will provide you with ideas and concepts to get you to think differently and help you better manage your money that can work in the real world rather than just relying on hypothetical projections or biased advice.

Finally, I personally use the strategies and concepts discussed in this book. That's because I practice what I preach.

Inside this book, you will learn:
- about the many financial misconceptions we have been taught;
- how the wealthy save and invest and why that knowledge is vital to how *you* should save and invest your own money;
- that saving and investing are *not* the same and why that distinction is important;
- why listening to and following the recommendations of Wall Street, the big brand-name and discount brokerage financial services firms, and many of the popular media pundits are not in your best interest;
- that the investment and financial strategies used to *accumulate* wealth for retirement are much different from the investment and financial strategies you should use to *distribute* wealth during retirement;
- the difference between *average* rates of return and *real* rates of return, and how it affects what you actually earn;
- how sequence of investment returns risk and market volatility can have a detrimental impact on your investment values, particularly during the retirement distribution phase;
- how to develop a retirement distribution plan that is not based on theory or hypotheticals but on facts and math;
- to think in terms of cash flow, not rate of return—because you can't spend rate of return; and
- that cash flow is what matters most and that is why cash flow is king!

All truth passes through three stages. First, it is ridiculed. Second, it is violently opposed. Third, it is accepted as being self-evident.
—Arthur Schopenhauer, philosopher

CHAPTER 1

Financial Misconceptions:
What You Believe to be True that May Not be True

If what you have been told to be the truth actually wasn't the truth, when would you want to know? Hopefully your answer is, "Right now!"

We are constantly bombarded with supposed "truths" and "facts," which are actually just opinions and perspectives, about almost everything from the foods we should eat to the best ways to exercise and, of course, how to save, invest, and manage our money. This is further exacerbated by the internet, where we can find all kinds of information from self-proclaimed "experts" giving their advice on anything and everything—advice which is often either incorrect, baseless, or just self-serving. Even worse is the belief that we are being provided with fair, accurate, and unbiased advice: "It's on the internet, so it must be true!" Unfortunately, this just isn't the case. Is it any wonder people are so confused?

You would think that with so much financial information available from so many sources we would all be wealthy or, at the very least, financially secure. But lack of wealth or financial security is not so much the result of what we don't know; it's the fact that what we believe to be true actually are not.

Even with all the easily accessible and available information, this abundance of information does not equate to knowledge. Knowledge is what we need to seek, not just information. Don't confuse the two. Obtaining knowledge can take time. It is the accumulation of information filtered through thorough research and, equally important, requires an open mind. You need to be willing to learn and understand all your available options and alternatives to help you make an informed decision that's in your best interest. Becoming knowledgeable is not always easy, that's for sure. Especially regarding financial advice.

Unfortunately, how most people have been taught to think about saving, investing, financial products, retirement planning, etc. has led many of them to come up short on their financial goals. They may have taken excessive and unnecessary risk that resulted in having to make needless sacrifices. This is because many people *don't know what they don't know!* They just *think* that they do as a result of all the false and misleading information they are being provided. That's because how you think determines your behavior. In other words, how you analyze and interpret the advice and information you are receiving, as well as the sources of this information, usually determines what conclusions you come away with and what choices you will make. Therefore, now is the time to start to think differently.

In order to think differently, you first have to see that what you think to be true, actually isn't true. Let's start by taking a look at many of the misconceptions you will frequently hear and tend to believe:

- Taking more risk earns you higher returns.
- The average rate of return is an accurate gauge of your investment performance.
- You can rely on dividends and interest for retirement income.
- Cash flow is only needed when you retire.
- When you borrow from a cash value life insurance policy, you are borrowing your own money.
- Cash value life insurance is more expensive than term life insurance.
- You will be in a lower tax bracket in retirement.
- You can live off less income in retirement.
- You can rely on the withdrawal rates recommended by most of the financial services industry.
- 401(k) plans are the ideal retirement account.
- 401(k) contributions (or traditional IRA contributions, if eligible) are a tax deduction.
- You save interest when paying cash instead of taking out a loan.
- Cheaper is better.
- The majority is always right (i.e., follow the crowd because they know best).
- I can get good financial and investment advice from my cousin, father, boss, accountant, etc.
- Wall Street and the big brand-name and discount brokerage financial services firms have the best money managers and investments, and they provide financial advice that's always in your best interest and most appropriate for you.
- Media pundits provide objective, real-world financial and investment advice that's right for each person's unique situation.

So many people have been exposed to these misconceptions for so long that they tend to believe them without always questioning them. They just accept them at face value. Let's look at each of these misconceptions a little more closely.

Taking more risk earns you higher returns. It's important to point out that this is not a guaranteed cause and effect. Taking more risk equates to just that: more risk. There certainly have been times throughout history where more risk resulted in higher returns; however, this is certainly not always the case and definitely a poor indicator to base future returns on. The fact is, there have also been times throughout history where more risk resulted in lower returns and even losses. Every investment prospectus has a disclaimer stating, "Past investment performance is not indicative of future investment performance." It's there for a reason! There are many factors that can affect investment performance, most of which are out of our control. Simply taking more risk to try to achieve higher returns is not a prudent investment strategy in and of itself. In fact, it's just a "hope and pray" strategy.

Of course, most of the financial services industry thrives off this strategy. That's because if you take more risk and your investment provides higher returns, you will be a happy camper. In fact, those in the financial services industry that focus their advice around investing in the stock market will often illustrate how much more money you will have in "x number of years" if you earn 2, 3, 4, 5 percent or higher rate of return. It certainly looks great on paper and can be quite convincing. After all, most people want the highest possible rate of return—with the least amount of risk, of course. However, when the markets go down (e.g., there is a major market correction or a bear market) or, there is simply an extended period of stagnate growth in the stock market (e.g., the lost decade of 2000-2009), taking more risk can completely backfire and hinder your ability to reach your financial goals.

Since most of the financial services industry has many people believing the idea of more risk equals higher returns, when the markets do drop, their "expert advice" is typically along the lines of: "just hold" or "ride it out." Then they'll often add, "After all, everyone is in the same boat." This sounds reasonable, right? Wrong! The truth is, more risk doesn't automatically equate to higher returns. It may appear that way when the markets are up, but it's certainly not the case when they are down. And, markets *do* go down. In Chapter 2, you will learn the math behind why more risk doesn't necessarily earn you higher returns.

The average rate of return is an accurate gauge of your investment performance. The average rate of return calculation[1] can be very misleading. The average rate of return is simply the average of returns an investment has provided over a given period. For example, if you invested $10,000, and the first year the investment went up 100 percent, and then the second year it went down 50 percent, your average rate of return would be 25 percent (100 minus 50 divided by 2 [years] equals 25). However, the more important questions to ask are "What is the value of my account after the second year?" and "Did I even make money?" Remember, your average rate of return was 25 percent. Sounds great, but the reality is, your account value is back to $10,000—exactly what you started with! (Keep in mind, we did not even factor in any fees.) In fact, one could argue that you even *lost* money. Why? Because, in hindsight, you could have simply put that $10,000 into some type of savings and at least earned *something*. (This is what's called opportunity cost, which I'll cover later.) Of course, this is an extreme example as most people aren't investing for only a two-year period, nor will they see a 100-percent gain one year and a 50-percent loss the next (at least they shouldn't). So, let's take a look at a much longer investment time horizon.

According to Crestmont Research (see chart below), the Dow Jones Industrial Average® (DJIA) from 1900 through 2017 has had an *average* rate of return of 7.4 percent. However, the *real* rate of return or *compounded* rate of return was only 5.1 percent (and this is before any fees and taxes). This is because the real rate of return inherently adjusts for the negative years as well as the volatility of the investment. Your real rate of return is what matters because that is what you, the investor, actually earns, and therefore, you should gauge your investment returns based on that calculation rather than on the average rate of return most of the financial services industry like to promote.

Furthermore, regarding average rates of return, many people assume that if

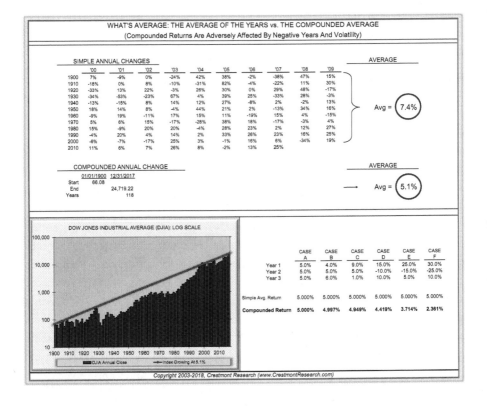

they project to earn a specific average rate of return, such as 7 percent per year, this is what they will actually earn—each and every year. However, this is not how the returns in the stock market are earned. For example, your investment account could be up 20 percent one year and then down 6 percent the next year. That is an average rate of return of 7 percent per year but clearly you did not earn 7 percent *each* year. The reality is that year-to-year stock market returns are random and unpredictable. This is very important to understand.

Look at the following S&P 500® index returns from 2001 through 2016.[2]

2016	11.93%
2015	1.31%
2014	13.81%
2013	32.43%
2012	11.93%
2011	2.07%
2010	14.87%
2009	27.11%
2008	−37.22%
2007	5.46%
2006	15.74%
2005	4.79%
2004	10.82%
2003	28.72%
2002	−22.27%
2001	−11.98%

As you can see, not one year had a rate of return of 7 percent, even though the average rate of return was 7 percent. The returns earned in the stock market are not constant, let alone reliable. They never are.

You can rely on dividends and interest for retirement income. Relying on dividends and interest can be risky. Let's first discuss dividends. Dividends are a source of cash flow. However, what happens when a company cuts or even stops paying out its dividend? It's important to realize that dividends are not guaranteed, even from the best of companies. If the dividend is cut or eliminated altogether, then what? You could sell the stock, but you probably would not want to since the price likely has dropped as a result of the dividend being cut or eliminated. Even if you did sell, where would you put the money from the sale to replace that reduced or lost dividend? You still have bills to pay and you still want to maintain your standard of living. So, what are your options? What will you have to sacrifice during your retirement?

The following demonstrates the risk of relying on dividends:

In 2008:

Sixty-eight companies in the S&P 500 alone cut their dividends with another 10 eliminating dividends altogether. (www.seekingalpha.com)

In 2009:

Poor economy puts dividend payments on track to decline by 22.6 percent this year, the most since 1938, S&P analyst says. (money.cnn.com)

Investors who count on dividend payments as a safe investment are getting hammered right along with share prices. (money.cnn.com)

In November 2017:

GE (General Electric), a company that has been a long-time staple in the American economy announced they were cutting their quarterly dividend… in half! (money.cnn.com)

Of course, the GE stock price dropped as a result. And let me point out, there was no economic crisis in 2017. If you were relying on the dividend from GE, this has now become a very serious problem for you.

What about interest earnings? We know they can provide cash flow too, but what if you base your retirement cash flow on interest rates that later drop? Your options are to either reduce your spending, if possible, or begin to withdraw from principal, which will now increase the risk of depleting your account. Of course, you could move your money into stocks or stock mutual funds that generate dividends, but I've already addressed the risk of that option. Remember, if you spend down your principal and your account eventually depletes to zero because you are withdrawing more than the interest earnings, you will then have zero interest earnings to generate cash flow. As a result, you will no longer receive retirement income from that account.

History of bank CD rates:

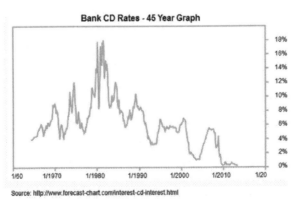

Bank CD Rates - 45 Year Graph

Source: http://www.forecast-chart.com/interest-cd-interest.html

Cash flow is only needed when you retire. This is not true at all because we *always* have a need for cash flow. Think about it. If you aren't retired, you are *already* receiving cash flow through paychecks from your employer or distributions from your business. This cash flow is then used to pay your bills, pay off debt, or to save and invest. The truth is, cash flow is a crucial component of every aspect of our lives, not just during retirement. In fact, it is a big part of why I wrote this book.

When it comes to saving and investing, we have been taught to focus on rates of return rather than on cash flow. However, when you fully understand how beneficial cash flow is when it comes to saving and investing, you'll be able to see that it can actually contribute tremendously toward your rate of return. That's because cash flow that is added back to your savings or investment account (i.e., reinvested) can help a great deal with the total growth of your account, far more than without cash flow. This is often referred to as compound interest. This, and *time*, are what makes compounding so powerful and why compound interest is often called the "eighth wonder of the world." The key though, is that the growth never stops and never loses value, which doesn't happen when investing in the stock market. And for this "phenomenon" to work, cash flow is required. Remember, regardless of what stage in life you're in, you should *always* be thinking in terms of cash flow.

When you borrow from a cash value life insurance policy, you are borrowing your own money. This is not true and often results in much confusion. The truth is that the money you borrow actually comes from the general assets of the life insurance company. Your cash value is simply used as collateral for the policy loan. This means that 100 percent of the cash value can still continue to grow. And, because you are borrowing from the assets of the insurance company and not from your own cash value, this is why the insurance company charges interest on the policy loan. This is very similar to a home equity loan, in that you are not actually borrowing *your own equity* from the home—you are borrowing from the general assets of the bank or credit union. Your equity remains in the home and is just used as collateral for the loan; the bank or credit union charges you interest on the loan. The fact that you are not borrowing your own money is an important distinction to understand.

Cash value life insurance is more expensive than term life insurance. This statement can be misleading. That's because most people are making an apples-to-oranges comparison of these two types of life insurance policies. But, that's only because of how they have been taught to think about them. What is important to understand is that the premiums maybe *higher* but that doesn't necessarily mean they are *more expensive*. In addition, the premiums may be higher in the early years; however, in later years, this certainly won't be the case. Let me explain. A cash value life insurance policy has a higher premium because it's structured to pay a death benefit whenever you die—even if that's at age 100 or later. It's sort of like a "lifetime term policy." As long as premiums are paid, the insurance company knows with certainty, that it will pay out a death benefit at some point, and therefore, it needs to structure the premium payments to prepare for that occurrence.

In contrast, a term life insurance policy is *only* structured to pay a death benefit if you die during the specific term period of the policy, such as 10, 20, or 30 years. The statistical risk to the insurance company paying out a death claim is far less with a term life insurance policy than a cash value life insurance policy, at least until around the age of 60. When comparing the cost of premiums, it's important to make sure you are making the appropriate or apples-to-apples comparison. For example, a 30-year term policy will have a higher premium than a 10-year term policy. This makes perfect sense, because the insurance company is at risk of paying a death benefit for 20 additional years with the 30-year term policy. The longer you live, the closer you are to death. That's just a fact that can't be denied. Does that mean the 10-year term policy costs less and is therefore the more appropriate type of term policy? Of course not! The appropriate comparison would be to compare the premium on the 30-year term policy to the premium on the 10-year term policy *plus* what the increasing premiums would be over the next 20 years. That's an apples-to-apples comparison.

Think what the premium would need to be on a term life policy to insure someone for 50, 60, or 70 years? Obviously, much more than even a 30-year term policy, right? Therefore, it's only common sense that the premiums on a cash value life insurance policy would be higher than a term life insurance policy. But stating that the premiums are more expensive would be inaccurate. Only in hindsight would we know which was the more expensive policy. For example, if the insured died within 10 years of a 10-year term life policy, that policy would have been less expensive than if the insured had a 20 or 30-year term policy and certainly less than a cash value policy. However, if the insured died 25 years later, the 10-year term life policy would be more expensive than a 20 or 30-year term life policy simply because the premium on the 10-year term policy would have increased after year 10. If the insured lived to average life expectancy, then *all* term life policies would have been far more expensive than a cash value life insurance policy.

Furthermore, cash value life insurance policies build cash value (thus, their name), whereas term life insurance policies do not. This is considered a savings component of the policy. For this savings to occur, additional cash flow (i.e., additional premium) is required above the cost of insurance. Therefore, to compare the cost of term life insurance and cash value life insurance simply based on the difference in premiums—especially initially—is an inappropriate and even misleading comparison.

Here are two analogies to help better understand:

1) Renting likely has a lower monthly payment than a mortgage, but this doesn't necessarily mean renting is cheaper. In the short-term, it may, but in the long-term, it's mostly likely not. Remember, with a mortgage you are working your way toward owning the home, and as a result, you are building equity (just like in a cash value life insurance policy). The mortgage may have a higher payment, but saying it costs more than renting is a misleading assertion.

2) When comparing a 15-year mortgage to a 30-year mortgage, no one says the 30-year mortgage is cheaper than the 15-year mortgage because the payments are lower. Most people understand that the very reason a 15-year mortgage has a higher monthly payment is because it allows the mortgage to be paid off much faster compared to a 30-year mortgage. In addition, you are building equity much faster than with a 30-year mortgage. In fact, for many people, these are the very reasons why they prefer a 15-year mortgage over a 30-year mortgage. It all goes back to how you think, doesn't it?

Keep in mind, neither type of life insurance—term or cash value—is better than the other. Either type of life insurance or both combined can be appropriate to help meet your specific financial and risk management objectives.

Since I am on the subject of life insurance, I have found that many people will "turn a blind eye" when it comes to life insurance, or for that matter, disability insurance and long-term care insurance too—that is, until it's needed. Unfortunately, it's too late then. Therefore, when it comes to life, disability, and long-term care insurance, I believe the most prudent approach is this: plan as if the insurance *will* be needed and hope that it never is. This means maximizing the amount of insurance you can reasonably obtain and don't cut corners because you *think* you are saving a few dollars. This is a much wiser way to think in order to protect you and your family.

You will be in a lower tax bracket in retirement. This is not necessarily true. This belief stems from a time when income tax rates were substantially higher. Yes, can you believe it? They actually were. Below is a chart reflecting the historical top federal income tax rates in the United States. Where do you see income tax rates headed in the future? Likely going up, correct? But aside from that, if you want your lifestyle in retirement to be the same as, or at least similar, to what you enjoy now, then it's highly likely that your tax bracket will be about the same, not lower. And, think about this: to be in a lower tax bracket in retirement would mean having to live off a lot less income during retirement. You wouldn't wish for that, would you? Finally, many of the tax deductions that helped lower your income while you were working may no longer be available when you retire. You must factor this, along with the potential for higher income tax rates, into your retirement distribution planning.

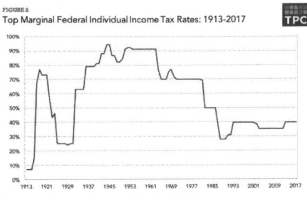

FIGURE 2
Top Marginal Federal Individual Income Tax Rates: 1913-2017

Source: "Historical Individual Income Tax Parameters," Tax Policy Center, May 5, 2017.

You can live off less income in retirement. Well, it depends. However, this is no longer a safe or prudent assumption. For one thing, you may still need or simply want the same amount of income in retirement as when you were working. Remember what I said in the previous misconception about maintaining your lifestyle in retirement? You may no longer have to save or invest for retirement, but those dollars may now need to be redirected to pay for other things, such as health insurance, long-term care insurance, or other expenses. Furthermore, you may want that cash flow to spend on travel or entertainment. After all, when you're retired, that's when you should be enjoying your additional free time and that may cost money. In addition, since you have no idea what your future tax liability will be and considering that tax rates may increase in the future, you may very well need more income just to cover the higher taxes.

You can rely on the withdrawal rates recommended by most of the financial services industry. It's likely too risky. When I became a financial advisor over 30 years ago, most of the financial services industry wasn't providing much information or guidance on creating reliable cash flow for retirement. To this day, they still aren't. Instead, the industry promoted how to get the highest rates of return, as they still do now. Back then, they used 12 percent *average* rates of return along with 7 percent annualized withdrawal rates in their retirement plan projections. These projections obviously looked great! A retiree could take plenty of retirement income and in 10, 15, or 20 years, for example, would continue to see a great deal of growth of their retirement assets. Can you imagine using those projections today? Worse, with all the volatility and market corrections we have experienced, imagine what your retirement assets and the income they were supposed to generate would look like today if you had actually used those projections.

The following is an example of what the typical retirement plan projections looked like then:

Initial retirement account value: $1 Million with a
7 percent annual withdrawal rate (cash flow of $70,000/year)

Year	Rate of return	Annual withdrawal	Year-end account balance
2000	12%	$70,000	$1,041,600
2001	12%	$70,000	$1,088,192
2002	12%	$70,000	$1,140,375
2003	12%	$70,000	$1,198,820
2004	12%	$70,000	$1,264,278
2005	12%	$70,000	$1,337,591
2006	12%	$70,000	$1,419,702
2007	12%	$70,000	$1,511,667
2008	12%	$70,000	$1,614,667
2009	12%	$70,000	$1,730,027
2010	12%	$70,000	$1,859,230
2011	12%	$70,000	$2,003,938
2012	12%	$70,000	$2,166,010
2013	12%	$70,000	$2,347,532
2014	12%	$70,000	$2,550,836
2015	12%	$70,000	$2,778,536
2016	12%	$70,000	$3,033,560

This looks really good, doesn't it? You started with an initial retirement account balance of $1 million, withdrew $70,000 a year for retirement income, and after 17 years your retirement account still grew to over $3 million.

Now, look what happens when you earn actual (real-world) stock market returns instead (next page):

**Initial retirement account value: $1 Million with a
7 percent annual withdrawal rate (cash flow of $70,000/year)**

Year	Rate of return[3]	Annual withdrawal	Year-end account balance
2000	−9.11%	$70,000	$845,277
2001	−11.98%	$70,000	$682,398
2002	−22.27%	$70,000	$476,017
2003	28.73%	$70,000	$522,665
2004	10.82%	$70,000	$501,644
2005	4.79%	$70,000	$452,272
2006	15.74%	$70,000	$442,441
2007	5.46%	$70,000	$392,776
2008	−37.22%	$70,000	$202,639
2009	27.11%	$70,000	$168,597
2010	14.87%	$70,000	$113,259
2011	2.07%	$70,000	$44,154
2012	15.88%	$70,000	$0
2013	32.43%	$70,000	$0
2014	13.81%	$70,000	$0
2015	1.31%	$70,000	$0
2016	11.92%	$70,000	$0

This doesn't look so good any more, does it? According to your retirement plan projections, you should have been able to withdraw $70,000 a year for the rest of your life *and* your retirement account should have grown substantially (to more than $3 million after 17 years). However, in the *real world,* you depleted your retirement account after just 12 years. That's what happens when you base your retirement plan off of unrealistic growth and withdrawal rate projections, and because your retirement account depleted to zero, there are no longer any withdrawals (i.e. cash flow) available to provide for your retirement. Of course, it certainly didn't help that the markets were negative the first few years. But, that's the point. In the real world, we don't know when the negative returns will occur and what sort of impact they will have. This is a risk called "sequence of returns risk" and will be discussed in more detail in Chapter 2.

The bottom line is, investing in the stock market will most likely not support those high rates of return or withdrawal rate projections. Because in real life, the markets don't go up 12 percent year after year (as you learned in the misconception: The average rate of return is an accurate gauge of your investment performance). Sure, some years the markets are up 12 percent or more, but some years they are not. Of course, those hypothetical projections certainly don't take into consideration any of the negative years. That's quite important to note because we have certainly seen negative years. Real-world results or occurrences can surely blow up the projections of any hypothetical retirement plan you may have been presented with.

Here is an interesting fact from this real-world example: The S&P 500® Index *average rate of return* during this period[4] was a positive 6.14 percent.

In time, the financial services industry prudently lowered those unrealistic rates of return and withdrawal rate projections. According to the financial services industry, a 9 to 10 percent rate of return and a 4 to 5 percent systematic withdrawal rate was eventually considered a more *reasonable* and *sustainable* projection in retirement. There was a period of time when those revised rates of return and withdrawal rates may have worked. However, as usual, times have changed. We now have historically low interest rates along with lower growth projections in the stock market. As of 2018, the projected growth rate in the stock market is 5 to 6 percent and the suggested withdrawal rate is now closer to 3 percent or less.

According to a Morningstar[5] study from 2013, a portfolio composition of 40 percent bonds and 60 percent stocks with a 2.8 percent inflation-adjusted withdrawal rate that could *potentially* last 30 years has a 90 percent success rate. Some financial articles have even suggested that retirees use these low systematic withdrawal rates of 3 percent or less with the caveat to protect against running out of retirement income by spending less in bad market years. Easy for them to say! First off, do you even have sufficient retirement assets to live off a 3 percent or less withdrawal rate? Second, most retirees can't just easily cut back on their spending. Third, we won't know the bad market years until *after* they've happened. By then it's a little too late to adjust your withdrawals. The truth is, those supposedly *safe* withdrawal rate assumptions can never account or adjust for how things in the *real world* will play out. Relying on them may put you at the very real risk of running of money and, as a result, no longer having retirement income.

401(k) plans are the ideal retirement account. They actually aren't as ideal as most people think they are. Here is a brief history: Over the years, 401(k) plans have grown to become immensely popular retirement accounts. Practically everyone talks about them and wants one. Their popularity began when the large corporations stopped offering pension plans, which were far more expensive than the 401(k) option. Also, smaller companies that never offered any type of retirement plan could easily offer a 401(k) plan to their employees. Wall Street got involved and started touting the opportunity for high rates of return by investing in the stock market through a 401(k). And finally, the tax-incentive (pre-tax contributions[6]) and the potential for a company match really sealed the deal for the 401(k)'s popularity.

The further appeal is that you are able to make larger contributions to a 401(k) than to an IRA (individual retirement account), and if you separate from your employer at age 55 (or older, but not yet age 59½) you could be eligible to take penalty-free withdrawals although, not many people are aware of this. The 401(k) is also very easy to contribute to, with contributions taken directly out of your paycheck. Likewise, when you start a new job that offers a 401(k), the employer will automatically enroll you in the plan and default your investment election to a target date mutual fund that's closest to your assumed retirement age of 65 (the plan's default election doesn't consider what *your* actual retirement age may be). For example, if you were going to be 65 in the year 2034, you'd be enrolled in the "Target 2035 Fund" or a similar name. A 401(k) can also be viewed as an attractive feature for young people starting out in the workforce who don't have much disposable income to save, as well as people of any age who find saving difficult. In these instances, the *convenience* of the 401(k) would seem to make sense. It's like a forced savings. However, don't use convenience as your crutch. You should look to save and invest, not because it's convenient or easy, but because it's the prudent thing to do. In addition, I believe it's very important to take responsibility by making a serious commitment to learning about all your options to save and invest for your future.

I've addressed the appeal of the 401(k); now let me address the problems. Even with the ease of making contributions and the other features I mentioned, 401(k) plans are far from perfect. In fact, they have numerous pitfalls that very few people realize, again, because of what they have been taught, which leads them to how they think. For example, most 401(k) plans offer a limited choice of investments and lack many core asset classes to select from in order to prudently diversify. In addition, many plans don't even offer the option of a dividend-paying mutual fund or some other type of investment that can generate reliable cash flow. Most 401(k) plans only offer growth mutual funds that pay little to no dividends. The problem with this is that dividends have historically been a key component of an investment's total return. The lack of available cash flow options doesn't benefit 401(k) participants.

I am not suggesting 401(k) plans should offer unlimited choices. However, they should at least offer enough core asset classes to diversify adequately, as well as offer investments that generate cash flow (e.g., dividends). This becomes more important as your account balance grows to tens of thousands, and certainly hundreds of thousands of dollars or more. Another pitfall with 401(k) plans is that most of the investment choices are linked to the stock market. What's the problem with that you ask? The problem is that you are forced to take market risk with really no other viable options to choose from. As you learned in the first misconception of this chapter, more risk doesn't always equate to higher returns. Also, many investors tend to base their investment decisions on their emotions. This often leads to making the wrong choices at the wrong time, such as selling after the markets have dropped. The other problem with having most of your investments linked to the stock market is their high correlation to each other. This means the investments (e.g., mutual funds) offered in the 401(k) plan will likely all go up or all go down in unison. This creates both volatility risk and volatility cost which you will learn more about in Chapter 2. The point is, you are forced to rely far too much on the performance of the stock market. Again, not everyone wants to, nor should, take on that much risk with all or most of their retirement money.

What about the highly promoted target date or lifecycle funds that are now in most 401(k) plans? Unfortunately, these aren't a solution either because they provide a false sense of security. These funds are set to run on autopilot, which is no way to manage your retirement account that's invested in the stock and bond market. They also may have hidden fees, lack adequate diversification, and worst of all, these funds are "one-size-fits-all" with regard to one's tolerance for risk. This simply isn't prudent because people have vastly different tolerances for risk which these generic investment portfolios don't or can't account for. The only other available options in 401(k) plans are usually some type of bond mutual fund or perhaps a stable value fund.[7] While these are geared toward conservative investors, with bond mutual funds in particular, you still have principal risk, and both bond mutual funds and stable value funds are subject to interest rate and inflation risk. When it comes to the investment options within most 401(k) plans, that's about all they offer. There just isn't much to really work with to create a properly diversified, let alone, low/non-market correlated retirement portfolio. (You will learn more about low/non-market correlation in Chapter 2.) It may not matter much when you first start out and there is not much money in your 401(k), but it will once you start to accumulate a lot more in the 401(k).

The reality is that many people view and use their 401(k) plan as their main retirement account. However, according to a CNBC.com article ("A brief history of the 401(k), which changed how Americans retire," Jan. 4, 2017), many of the early proponents of the 401(k) have said it was never designed to be the primary retirement tool.

In addition, the Economic Policy Institute recently declared the 401(k) "a poor substitute" for the defined benefit pension plans many workers once primarily relied on, which provided a fixed payout for employees at retirement, and which have now become increasingly rare. "The great lie is that the 401(k) was capable of replacing the old system of pensions," former American Society of

Pension Actuaries head Gerald Facciani tells *The Journal*. "It was oversold."

John Wasik of *Forbes* wrote on the history of the defined contribution system: "The 401(k) plan was never meant to be a mainstream pension plan and, from our perspective is a poor substitute for one. It's a voluntary program that was intended to supplement retirement savings—one of those quirky little options in the byzantine tax code that employers seized upon as a way to save money while pretending that they were doing the right thing by their employees."

Even the so-called "father of the 401(k)," Ted Benna, says with some regret that he "helped open the door for Wall Street to make even more money than they were already making."

When it comes to providing retirement income during the distribution phase, the 401(k) is even worse. That's because it is not designed to provide retirement income or cash flow, certainly not reliable and definitely not guaranteed. Typically, your only distribution option with a 401(k) is a systematic withdrawal. Chapter 2 will explain the pitfalls of using systematic withdrawals as your retirement income distribution strategy.

With few exceptions[8] you are probably better off rolling over your 401(k) into an IRA when you're eligible to do so (e.g., you leave your employer, you turn age 59½ and take an "in-service withdrawal," if available; and of course, you retire).

With an IRA, you have virtually unlimited savings and investment choices. You can therefore properly diversify by including asset classes that are not likely available in your 401(k) plan. You can also include low/nonmarket correlated investment options that don't always go up and down in unison, which can help lower volatility risk as well as volatility cost. And perhaps most important, you can take advantage of investments and financial products that provide reliable—even guaranteed—cash flow for retirement income. After all, that is really the primary objective of a retirement plan.

So, by all means, contribute to a 401(k) plan if your employer offers a matching contribution—it's free money. And, if you determine some of your retirement contributions should be made with pre-tax dollars, then a 401(k) can make sense as well. However, I would then strongly consider allocating the rest of your money to accounts that offer other types of savings, investments, and financial products that the 401(k) doesn't. An independent financial advisor can provide you with options that are appropriate for you.

Ultimately, your goal is to save as much as possible for retirement in such a way as to: (1) maximize your total return potential without excessive risk and (2) provide the maximum amount of after-tax retirement income that provides the most flexibility and control of your money. Now that is an ideal retirement plan! As such, you should now see that the 401(k) is not as ideal as it's made out to be.

Remember, it was never meant to be your *sole* retirement plan in the first place. It can certainly be a *part* of your plan to save and accumulate money for retirement, but it certainly should not be the *only* plan or even the primary plan.

401(k) contributions (or traditional IRA contributions, if eligible) are a tax deduction. This is not accurate because these contributions are actually a *tax deferral*. There is a distinct difference. A tax deduction reduces your taxes for that given tax year without the expectation that you will have to eventually pay the tax at some future date. Mortgage interest, property taxes, and charitable contributions are examples of actual tax deductions. On the other hand, a 401(k) contribution (or traditional IRA contribution, if eligible) is simply a tax deferral. You have the option to either pay tax on the contribution now (i.e., in the current year of the contribution) or in the future (i.e., when it's withdrawn). And if *you* don't, then your beneficiaries will.[9]

When determining whether or not to make a pre-tax contribution, keep in mind that the main purpose of contributing toward retirement is not for a tax deferral. It's to help maximize your eventual *after-tax* retirement income. This should always be your primary focus. Therefore, you should consider both the pros and cons of tax deferral of your contributions within your own retirement plan. For example, would you be better off contributing to a Roth IRA or Roth 401(k) which are after-tax instead of pre-tax, but withdrawals are tax-free? Or, perhaps you should consider allocating some of your retirement contributions to other types of accounts completely outside of a 401(k) and/or IRA.

You save interest when paying cash instead of taking out a loan. This is not as obvious as you may think. That's because there is more to this financial decision than just the amount of interest you pay out if you borrow or the amount of interest you think you save if you pay cash. Let me explain. When you take out a loan (e.g., a car loan or a home mortgage), most people tend to look only at the amount of interest they will (or did) pay out to determine the cost of the loan. For example, a 5-year car loan of $30,000 with a 5 percent interest rate will have incurred a total of $3,968[10] in interest (total payments were $33,968 of which $3,968 was interest). One might conclude that paying off the loan early (before 5 years) would save them interest or that paying cash for the car would save *all* the interest. However, this is not the whole story.

The deeper reality is, whether you pay cash or take out a loan for *any* purchase, there is always going to be a *cost* to you. That's because you either pay interest for having a loan or mortgage or you forego earning interest because your cash was removed from the account where it could have earned interest or been invested for potential growth. This is called opportunity cost, and you can't avoid it. This also applies for any extra or pre-payments, including bi-weekly mortgage payments, you make toward paying off any type of loan early. It's important to understand how opportunity cost impacts you and factor it into your financial choices. The fact is, opportunity cost does matter. It's real money that is lost.

Should You Prepay or Not Prepay?

When clients ask me if they should make extra payments toward their mortgage or loan (or pay it off entirely), I always respond by saying, "It depends." It depends on a lot of factors, not just how much interest will be paid out to the lender. As you just learned, you have to factor in opportunity cost. However, everyone's situation is different, and there is no one-size-fits-all solution. Therefore, I follow up "It depends" with "If you look at it purely from a financial and tax perspective, then we have to see what interest rate you are currently paying on the loan, adjust for any applicable tax deductions, and then compare it to the interest or investment rate of return, net of taxes, you can get by saving or investing the money instead."

Financial and tax wise, it generally doesn't make sense to prepay or pay off a low-interest rate loan early especially if you can deduct the interest which helps to reduce the cost on the interest you pay. However, some people just don't like having any debt at all regardless of the financial or tax benefits provided. Having no debt helps them sleep better at night knowing they do not owe anything and do not have a commitment of outgoing cash flow payments every month. It's peace of mind for them. Therefore, looking at the situation holistically, not just financially, there is not necessarily a single right or wrong answer applicable to everyone.

Note: Of all the misconceptions discussed so far, the following are the most important to understand and to beware of.

Cheaper is better. If "cheaper is better," then what about "you get what you pay for?" Quality and value for your money are what matter most—at least they should. We all have bought something at some time that was the least expensive only to find that the item or product was inferior. It just ended up being a waste of money. You then may have gone out and purchased the higher-priced item, which you realized was actually much better quality. For many, it's a hard lesson learned. (Unfortunately, not everyone learns this lesson.) When it comes to your finances and investments, it is just as important to remember "cheaper doesn't equal better." Let's go into this a bit more.

There is certainly a lot of hype around the belief that the lowest fees and expenses are always best. Charles Schwab, TD Ameritrade, and Fidelity, just to name a few, have promoted the "cheaper is better" mantra, and it has been quite profitable for them. It's an "easy" sales pitch. And of course, there is Vanguard, the pioneer and leader of low-cost investing. However, we must remember that cost is a relative term. All things being equal, then yes, you most certainly want the lower-cost option. For example, if Investment A has a similar or equivalent investment objective, degree of volatility, and investment performance to Investment B, yet Investment B has a lower management fee or expense ratio, then you'd certainly choose Investment B over Investment A. But all things are not always equal. If Investment A is actually less risky or volatile than Investment B, then even with a higher management fee, Investment A may be the more appropriate option for you. Perhaps Investment A offers a higher dividend rate or provides some type of guarantees. In that case too, Investment A may be worth paying a higher fee for those desired benefits and features. The point is, cost, fees, expenses, etc. can't be looked at in a vacuum. The investment or financial product with the lowest fees is not always the best or most appropriate choice. Rather than just asking, "What are the fees?" the real question you should be asking is, "What am I *getting* for the fees I am paying?" Remember, there is no free lunch. You'll learn more in Chapter 3 (How the Wealthy Save and Invest, and Why You Should Follow Their Philosophy), that *value for your money* is what you should be seeking.

Furthermore, there may be other fees or costs related to your investments or financial products that aren't always reflected or transparent such as in an investment prospectus.[11] Here are some examples of these "hidden" costs. One is trading costs. Trading costs are incurred when the mutual fund or investment manager buys and sells the positions held in the mutual fund or investment. Generally, the more positions in the mutual fund or investment that are bought and sold (i.e., traded) the higher the trading costs that are incurred. These trading costs, in most instances, are passed onto the investor.

Another example is volatility cost. Volatility cost resulting from market volatility which is fluctuations in share prices of stocks traded on the stock market can be a real cost that impacts the value of your portfolio over time. In fact, it can actually be more costly than the operating expenses and/or management fees you are already being charged. The higher the volatility of the investment, the higher the volatility cost you may potentially incur.

Let's look at an example:

For the period January 1, 1998 through December 31, 2008, the average rate of return of the S&P 500® index was 3.16 percent. (Remember what you have learned about average rate of return.) When adjusting for market volatility, the real rate of return was only 0.96 percent.[12] That's more than a 2 percent cost to you on your investment portfolio just from market volatility.

Now, go back to the comparison of Investment A and Investment B from above. Investment B has a lower operating expense or management fee than Investment A. However, Investment B is subject to much more volatility than Investment A. By factoring in *all* applicable costs and expenses (both transparent and nontransparent), during a period of market volatility, Investment A ends up with more money in the account than Investment B. Therefore, does it really matter that Investment B has a lower operating expense or management fee? Of course, it doesn't. Investment B may seem to cost less on the surface, but you certainly shouldn't base your decision solely on that premise alone. Keep in mind, this is just one of many possible factors you want to consider when choosing an appropriate investment or financial product.

Many media pundits also preach the cheaper is better mantra. However, they don't always practice what they preach. For example, in an interview with Suze Orman, *New York Times* journalist Deborah Solomon asked Orman: "What do you do with your money?" Suze replied, "Save it and build it in municipal bonds (notice she said *save it, not invest it,* regarding her money). I buy zero-coupon municipal bonds, and all the bonds I buy are triple-A-rated and insured so that even if the city goes under, I get my money. I take a little lower interest rate to make sure my bonds are 100 percent safe and sound."

Quite interesting, don't you think? She is in effect paying a fee[13] and knowingly incurring a higher cost for the benefit of safety. It would certainly be cheaper for her (and as a result, she would earn a higher rate of return) to forego insuring those bonds. But she clearly wants to eliminate risk, even though there is a cost to do so. Orman is receiving a benefit for the additional cost of insuring the bonds, isn't she? That is exactly how you should look at it as well, especially with regard to the concepts and strategies I am presenting throughout this book. Therefore, do what Suze Orman does—protect your money—and not what she says.

The Added Financial Value When Working with a Financial Advisor

As a financial advisor, I am compensated for the advice I provide. If someone believes they can do a better job than I can, I don't feel the need to try to convince them otherwise. There are far too many people who want and need independent and objective advice and who are willing to pay a fair and reasonable compensation for it. Those are the people I choose to focus my time and energy on.

Just as there are people who can change the oil in their car, build a deck in their backyard, or remodel their own kitchen, there are also people who simply can't or don't want to do it themselves. In fact, it may actually be more beneficial and provide you with a better value to hire someone who can provide such services for you. It may be for any number of valid reasons. Here are some reasons why: perhaps you may not have the time or you simply prefer not doing it yourself; you may simply not have the ability or knowledge; or your time may be better spent on something else. (Opportunity cost applies to your time as well.)

Hiring an expert or professional can save you time, save you from making costly mistakes, and yes, even save you money. Quite frankly, they likely will do a much better job as well. So, don't be afraid to outsource. In fact, I personally adhere to this philosophy.

Even Vanguard, the mutual fund giant that has built an investment empire by providing and marketing lower-cost mutual funds and investments, recognizes the value of hiring a financial advisor. Vanguard's own research[14] concluded that a financial advisor can potentially add up to 3 percent in *net return* to a client's investment portfolio. Their analysis was based on the financial advisor's ability to provide actual value in numerous ways. These included asset allocation strategies, cost-effective investment recommendations, and, most importantly, behavioral coaching. This last element means helping the client through the decision-making process, ensuring the client feels comfortable with investment selections, and advising the client to avoid making financial decisions based on their emotions but rather to stick to the plan the financial advisor created—essentially, providing prudent discipline and guidance along the way. When you consider these factors into the client-advisor relationship, you can see how the decision to not use a financial advisor simply to save on a fee can actually cost you more.

Therefore, don't think in terms of "cheaper is better." Instead, think in terms of "What am I getting for what I am paying for?" and "Am I getting value from that?" To paraphrase the old British adage: "Don't be penny wise and dollar foolish."

The majority is always right (i.e., follow the crowd because they know best). This is generally false especially when it relates to investment and financial advice. There once was a time when the majority thought the earth was flat, but the majority was clearly wrong. And not long ago, the consensus was that real estate values always went up and you couldn't lose value. Again, the majority was wrong. Unfortunately, when it comes to investment and financial advice, most people seem to follow what "everyone else" is doing. For example, when the stock market is soaring, it seems to motivate many people to invest more in the stock market. In fact, many people can't seem to invest fast enough. They feel they are missing out. Then, when the stock market is tanking and "everyone" is apparently selling, many people can't get out of it fast enough. They're afraid they might lose it all. But history has consistently shown us that following the crowd is not a prudent financial or investment strategy. Sadly, history has also shown us that most people haven't learned this lesson. One of the best examples of why we should not follow the crowd or believe the majority is always right is to look at Warren Buffett, who is considered one of the best stock investors and is one of the world's richest people. In his book, *Warren Buffett's Management Secrets*, it was revealed that one of his trademarks is to go against the trend and walk alone instead of doing what others do. He dared to challenge the norm by choosing to be different. He invested when no one else would and pulled out when everyone else was investing and feeling exuberant. His approach and results teach us that he wouldn't be as successful as he is if he had decided to go with the crowd.

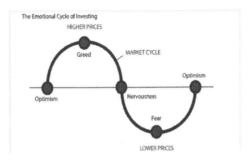

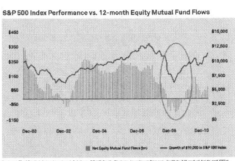

Vertical lines represent Net Equity Mutual Fund Flows
Horizontal line represents Growth of $10,000 in S&P 500® index

I can get good financial and investment advice from my cousin, brother, father, boss, CPA, etc. Perhaps, but not very likely. People have sometimes told me what their "smart" or "investment savvy" friend, relative, boss, or colleague at work is doing with their money. My response to them is simple: "It may be right for them but may not be right for you." Furthermore, how and where are they getting their advice? For all you know, they could be getting lousy advice and it's only working because of dumb luck or fortunate timing. And now, they are passing that not so great advice on to you and, just your bad luck, it doesn't work for you. Not to mention, they may be taking a lot more risk than you would prefer to take or you may not even be aware of the risks. Remember that their circumstances, goals, objectives, risk tolerance, etc. is likely to be very different from yours. You need to determine what's most appropriate for *you* and not listen to or follow what others are doing without thorough research. (Also, remember Warren Buffett's strategy mentioned previously.)

Your certified public accountant (CPA) is also not someone from whom you should be seeking financial planning or investment advice from. CPAs are professionals educated and trained in accounting and taxation, neither of which qualifies them as an expert in financial and investment planning advice. I work with and know many CPAs, and the honest ones acknowledge this fact. CPAs are great professionals to work with and can be a very valuable resource, just so long as you utilize them for what they have been trained in and not expect (or ask) them to advise outside of that scope.

Some CPAs offer financial and investment planning in addition to their tax and accounting services. However, the truth is a CPA can't competently do both. Being a financial advisor or CPA are both full-time professions. Each require devoting their time and attention to their clients; they must also spend considerable hours on continuing education. During tax season, do you actually think your CPA can be fully attentive or committed to his or her financial planning and investment clients? Not very likely. Tax season lasts for months and consumes almost all of the CPA's time and focus. Think about it this way—would you hire someone for legal advice or medical advice who practices as both a physician and attorney? Of course not! Therefore, don't short change yourself. Make sure you hire a full-time, fully dedicated independent financial advisor and not a CPA who attempts to do both financial advising and tax services.

Wall Street and the big brand-name and discount brokerage financial services firms have the best money managers and investments, and they provide financial advice that's always in your best interest and most appropriate for you. I have studied and researched the practices of these firms for many years and there is absolutely no evidence to support this. Unfortunately, many people follow their advice without truly understanding the risks, potential repercussions, or any of the alternatives available to them.

Many people also tend to believe that because Wall Street and the big brand-name and discount brokerage firms have supposedly hired and trained the top candidates from the most prestigious business schools, they will be the most successful money managers and will develop the "best" investment portfolios. There is also the fallacy that these firms have a "specialized" or "proprietary" investment strategy that's better than anyone else's. This is simply not true.

The truth is, they don't have a magic formula. No one does, because there is no magic formula. There is simply no truth that they can do any better than anyone else when it comes to financial advice and investing your money. In fact, all they do is invest most, if not all, of your money into the stock or bond market and then subject you to a high degree of market volatility and risk in the hope of providing you with high returns. Of course, you'll likely be quite content when the stock market is up, but during periods of extreme volatility or during a bear market for example, you will likely find it's more than you can tolerate. Plus, the volatility risk that they subject you to isn't even supported by the math. You'll read more about this in Chapter 2. Furthermore, they will most likely charge you high fees or subject you to hidden fees that do not even provide you with any value or benefit. They are notorious for this.

This also results in ongoing revenue or cash flow for them. Nothing inherently wrong with that, but think about it, Wall Street and the big brand-name and discount brokerage firms have a cash flow strategy, not a rate of return strategy. This is certainly much different from what they preach to us, isn't it? Unfortunately, other savings, investments, or financial products that are not tied to the stock market are seldom, if ever, offered. That's because these firms' primary source of revenue is derived, in a multitude of ways, from the stock market. Therefore, they have no incentive to look outside the scope of the stock market. The good news is that you will be introduced to some of the savings, investments, and financial products that can provide you with cash flow in later chapters in this book so you can have a cash flow strategy—not a rate of return strategy—just like Wall Street and the big brand-name and discount brokerage firms.

The Illusion of Independence

The investment representatives who work for these Wall Street or big brand-name and discount brokerage firms will claim that they are independent and can provide you with any type of investment or financial product. This is quite misleading. For example, when these representatives are asked for their opinion about certain investments or financial products that are not on their approved or preferred offering list, their response will generally be something like this: "Yes, we can offer those investments or financial products too. However, we don't like or recommend them (for whatever reason they give)." I hear about these conversations quite often. First, the statement that they don't recommend them is because they are probably not allowed to. At the very least, they are strongly discouraged from doing so. That's because if the investment or financial product being asked about is not part of their firm's primary profit center, they have no incentive to recommend it. Also, keep in mind, these investment representatives aren't providing you with their own independent advice. They are just passing on what the firm they work for wants you to do with your money. They are simply the messenger. Furthermore, when they are asked about other investments or savings options, such as real estate, annuities, or cash value life insurance, these investment representatives will usually give you an answer that is likely inaccurate or even misleading, although, it may not always be intentionally inaccurate or misleading. It's important to understand that they likely have very little knowledge about other investments or financial products other than what they have been trained by Wall Street, the big brand-name, or discount brokerage firms they work for (which is nothing or very little). The truth is, they are just passing on to you this "bad" or misleading information simply because that is all that they have been taught.

In Whose Best Interest Is the Investment Representative Working?
Most of these Wall Street or big brand-name and discount brokerage firms compensate their investment representatives based on sales goals. It's less about financial planning and investment advice and more about generating new assets and accounts. Depending on the firm, their plan or advice to help meet your financial goal is typically some proprietary stock portfolio or in-house annuity or insurance policy that is most profitable for *them*. They will usually tout their advice as being specific to your situation, but it still seems to always come back to a recommendation of one of their proprietary investments or financial products. It's the one-size-fits-all investment or financial plan.

Furthermore, the branch manager or supervisor who is training and managing these investment representatives also have compensation incentives based on the proprietary investments and financial products they sell. Unfortunately, this is quite common and can certainly lead to biased advice.

The discount brokerage firms, in particular, will often claim that they offer unbiased investment advice at little to no cost. Fidelity, for example, is notorious for this. In the past, I have actually had clients receive calls from representatives at Fidelity saying that they can have their 401(k) rollover or lump sum pension managed with no fees. The scary thing is that many people believe them. After all, who wouldn't want something for nothing? But let's not forget that there is no such thing as a free lunch; we get what we pay for. Also, think about this: who do you think is paying for those commercials, marketing and advertising, call centers, large office buildings, and other operating expenses? Their customers are ultimately paying, that's who! Therefore, it can't be free.

The *Wall Street Journal* interviewed dozens of former employees of the three largest discount brokers based on assets—Fidelity, Charles Schwab Corp., and TD Ameritrade Holding Corp—all known for supposedly bringing low-cost investing to the average person ("Advisors at Leading Discount Brokers Win Bonuses to Push Higher-Priced Products," January 10, 2018, WSJ.com). Nearly everyone interviewed said the compensation practices encouraged workers to sell financial products that were more lucrative for the employee and the firm and that cost their customers more in fees. According to a former branch manager at Fidelity Investments, "Clients hear the representative doesn't work on commissions, and they think that means the rep doesn't work on incentives." Likewise, a Fidelity advisor said, "If a customer had at least $50,000, you had to lead off by recommending a Fidelity-managed account, and if you didn't, you had to have a reason for it."

You probably never heard of the term "sandbagging" as it relates to the investment industry. Sandbagging is when an investment representative has met his or her quota of new investments for the quarter and intentionally delays accepting and/or investing new money until the start of the next quarter. According to the same *Wall Street Journal* article, this was said to have occurred at TD Ameritrade. This clearly benefits the advisor but certainly doesn't benefit the customer.

The truth is, there is no proof that you are getting any better advice or investment returns by using any of these discount brokerage firms, while there is ample proof of conflicts of interest. Also, you may think you are paying less in fees with these firms, but this is not always the case. And even when it may seem to be the case, I've already explained that cheaper is not always better. There are no short-cuts, especially when it comes to financial advice. My suggestion is to use these discount brokerage firms in the situation where you already know which stocks you want to buy. Simply set up an account and make your trades online. Other than that, *caveat emptor* (buyer beware*).*

These discount brokerage firms also like to refer to their investment representatives as financial advisors. I have been a financial advisor for over 30 years. I definitely know what a financial advisor is, and these representatives certainly are not. In addition to calling them financial advisors, they are often given titles like "retirement specialist," even though they aren't, at least not in the true sense of the term. A standardized, company-run training program doesn't qualify anyone to be a financial advisor, retirement specialist, or any sort of financial expert.

Furthermore, they often read off a script when you contact their call center and finally (and to me, most concerning), once their 9-5 work day ends, they are off the clock. Meaning that any further interest in you and your finances is off the clock as well. They just don't have a long-term vested interest in you or your money. How can they? And, why would they? They have no incentive to be creative, think outside the financial box, or challenge conventional thinking on your behalf. Not only are they not trained to, they are not paid to. If there is a better or more appropriate way, you'll certainly never hear about. Is this really how you want to receive financial advice? I am certain it's not.

These discount brokerage firms also like to promote themselves as wealth managers. This, too, is misleading. Let me strongly emphasize that they are not wealth managers. Investing your money in the stock market is only one aspect of wealth management, but it certainly doesn't entail everything that a true wealth manager provides. It's just a marketing gimmick. Therefore, beware of these types of companies that call themselves wealth managers when in reality they are anything but.

All of this conflicting, inaccurate, and misleading advice is one thing. What's worse though, is the impression given that any of these Wall Street and big brand-name or discount brokerage firms actually care about you and your financial goals. You've seen their advertisements and commercials. However, don't let any of this fool you—it's just very creative marketing on their part. As long as you give them your money and continue to give them more and more of your money, they will act as if they care and that you matter to them. Some even place their customers into clever categories, such "private client," to make them feel special or appreciated. Of course, to "qualify" and maintain this "special" status, customers are often required to keep a certain minimum balance with them that can amount to tens of thousands of dollars. They will also try to entice you to move your assets over to them in order to qualify for a supposed better interest rate on a loan or mortgage with their in-house lending department. But the sneaky truth is, they are just looking to "lock up" your money with them. To them, it's only about gathering new assets and accounts. Meanwhile, you have lost control and flexibility of your money. It may not seem that way on the surface, but that's exactly what's going on.

What these firms do care about are their shareholders and senior management (i.e., themselves). Their top priority is to look out for their own profitability and future growth opportunities. In fact, you're just a number to them, one of thousands of accounts needed to help reach their own compensation goals and incentives. They are ultimately looking out for what's in their best interest, not yours.

Wall Street and the big brand-name and discount brokerage firms have a long history of greed and it has cost investors plenty over the years. In fact, let's not forget their major roles in our past two financial crisis alone, which led to investors losing a substantial amount of their hard-earned money—not to mention the many who lost their jobs, homes, and more. Here are just some of many examples:

- The dot-com crisis (2000–2002)
- The stock market and real estate crash (2008) followed by the Great Recession
- The collapse of Merrill Lynch in 2008—which still managed to pay out billions of dollars in bonuses to their top executives
- Lehman Brothers and Bear Stearns bankruptcy
- JP Morgan's infamous trading activities that resulted in the loss of billions of dollars
- Morgan Stanley's $13 billion settlement in 2017 for overbilling clients' managed accounts
- Wells Fargo creating 3.5 million phony credit cards and bank accounts without customer consent

In addition, let's not forget the countless smaller settlements with their customers that don't make the headlines, or the substantial fines and penalties imposed by the regulatory agencies that oversee them.

I don't understand why people continue to trust them and allow them to manage their money. Haven't they learned their lesson yet?

Remember this harsh fact: Wall Street and the big brand-name and discount brokerage firms aren't taking any risk with *their* money. They are taking risk with *your* money. It's always easier to take more risk with someone else's money than your own, isn't it? They have nothing to lose. But you certainly do. If you take away anything from this section, take away that fact. Jeff Titak,[15] CFP®, RICP®, states it best:

> "Initially excited to be working in the financial services industry, I was shocked and disgusted to find a world that was driven largely by sales quotas, corporate initiatives, and a lack of transparency. The structure was essentially designed to work against clients and not in their best interests."

What should you do? Hire an independent financial advisor who is not affiliated with Wall Street, a big brand-name financial firm, or a discount brokerage firm. The advice and recommendations can then be about what's in *your* best interest and not the large financial services firm. Plus, it's always a good idea to support small businesses. After all, small businesses are the backbone of our economy, not these large corporations.

Media pundits provide objective and real-world financial and investment advice that's right for each person's unique situation. I have found neither "objective" nor "real-world" to be true. Media pundits are a major contributor and influence regarding financial information and advice to the consumer. Think about all the financial and business shows on television and radio, the multitude of financial and investment magazines, and the newspapers with frequent financial articles and topics. It's a 24-hour, 7-days-a-week devotion to providing financial and investment advice to their audience. It's "big business" with a lot of careers and money at stake!

The reality is that these media pundits can say virtually *anything* with little to no accountability. They have no financial regulatory oversight to contend with, such as the Securities and Exchange Commission (SEC) or Financial Industry Regulatory Authority (FINRA). Therefore, how do you really know if their advice is current, accurate, or even unbiased? What is their filtering or due diligence process on investment and financial products? Do they even have a process? And more important, is any of their advice even right for you? Think about it: they are literally reaching out to millions of people every day. Financial advice never has been and never can be one-size-fits-all. But yet, that's all they can offer. They often attempt to make their advice and ideas suit their whole audience. The truth is, however, people react to and handle things very differently. For example, diets and exercise programs can have varying results for different people. Medications work well for some people and don't work at all for others, or, some people have severe side effects from medications while others have none. Likewise, people handle the consumption of alcohol very differently. The point is, speaking into a microphone to a huge audience cannot offer the specific type of advice and ongoing guidance that each person requires and should expect. This is true whether it's exercise, diet, medical, or financial advice. As much as they try, it just can't be done. People's individual situations, needs, goals, and risk tolerances are very different.

Furthermore, you may think these media pundits are unbiased simply because they are on television or the radio. And you aren't paying them either, so what's the harm in free advice? (Unless of course, you purchase their books, CDs, DVDs, etc.—though, remember the Suze Orman prepaid debit card she promoted and the fiasco that followed?) But the truth is, they are not financial advisors or even financial fiduciaries. Nor are they true consumer advocates—not when they are ultimately selling something for a profit. At the most honest and basic level, they are marketing promoters and entertainers. In a *Forbes* article written by Charles Sizemore, he states, "*Expert* can be something a subjective term, and a lot of the advice that is shared over the airwaves can do more harm than good." He further writes, "Financial punditry is not charity. Every person you see expressing an opinion on TV, radio, or in print has a motive." He continues, "You shouldn't take advice from a pundit who refuses to acknowledge when they are wrong—or to acknowledge the possibility that they could be wrong." I couldn't agree more with that statement.

The Media Pundits' Illusion of High Rates of Return

Besides the fact that these media pundits simply can't offer personalized advice, another very real concern is that they constantly talk about earning high (double-digit) rates of return.

Suze Orman and Dave Ramsey, two popular media pundits, often talk about earning high rates of return in the stock market by investing in mutual funds, for example. Dave Ramsey has stated that he will use a 12 percent assumed average rate of return in his financial projections.[16] (As you previously read, and will read more in Chapter 2, average rates of return can be very misleading and can overstate what your real rate of return actually is). To try and achieve a 12 percent average rate of return on your money, you would have to invest 100 percent of it into the stock market, which is precisely what he recommends. No allocation to fixed income (e.g., bonds). To make matters worse, his recommended withdrawal rate for retirees is 8 percent[17] (is he still living in the 1980s or 90s?). This is just absurd and certainly not very realistic. But again, because he is a media pundit, he can say virtually anything he wants without any regulatory oversight or supervision unlike myself and other licensed and regulated financial advisors.

Suze Orman doesn't even seem to practice what she preaches. She has publicly stated that she has very little of her own net worth in the stock market or any of the high-risk and highly volatile investments (e.g., mutual funds) she is always touting.[18] She has publicly stated that much of her net worth is in municipal bonds. It doesn't appear she has the same confidence in the growth potential of the stock market for her own money as she has for your money, does she? She is certainly not willing to take the risk, is she? But according to her, it's okay for you to take that risk.

How can they claim these high rates of return? Because of something you learned earlier—they are using the average rate of return instead of the more appropriate real rate of return calculation. That's why Ramsey can say 12 percent (though, still misleading) because, from 1900 through 2016, the average rate of return of the S&P 500® index was 11.54 percent. However, when the more accurate calculation of the real rate of return is used, the S&P 500® index return was only 9.71 percent.[19] Remember, this is before any fees or income taxes. In addition, the Dow Jones Industrial index® (the Dow) real rate of return has been only 5.1 percent over the past 117 years.[20] Even during the last two decades ending December 31, 2016, the S&P 500® index 20-year real rate of return was just 8.35 percent, before any fees and taxes. As you can see, this is a far cry from the 12 percent that these pundits promote. I can't say this enough—the real rate of return is what matters because you, as an investor, don't earn the average rate of return.

Furthermore, earning high annual rates of return are neither constant nor sustainable and striving for them incur a high degree of risk. The same goes for using high withdrawal rates when investing in the stock market. Therefore, they certainly should not be relied upon or used in your projections. Unfortunately, many people buy into this false assertion (and implied promise) of such high rates of return. Who wouldn't want to believe them? After all, their pitch is quite convincing, and they couldn't be on TV or the radio if they weren't telling the truth, right? Wrong!

We shouldn't accept at face value this generalized financial advice that's so easily accessible on TV, radio, and other mass media outlets. The truth is, the sooner you divest yourself of the opinions and views of these media pundits—as well as Wall Street, the big brand-name and discount brokerage firms the better off you'll be. It's not easy. Wall Street, the big brand-name and discount brokerage firms, and media pundits are seemingly everywhere and they can be quite persuasive. Instead, work with an independent financial advisor who is willing to present the pros and cons to you in an unbiased manner based on your own personal situation. This will help you obtain the proper knowledge over just having information that may be misleading, inaccurate, or even biased. You can then have the confidence to implement what is most appropriate for you and you alone.

Of course, not all media pundits are this way. There are some who do take a different approach with their audiences. Terry Savage, for one, is a nationally known personal finance columnist and author who I have found to be honest and sincere in educating people on personal finance. I find her to be open-minded and fair, and she doesn't shun certain financial products simply because they aren't stocks, mutual funds, or exchange-traded funds as many of the others constantly do. We would all be better off if more of the media provided financial information in context the way Savage does.

Instead of listening to Ramsey and Orman, and many of the others, you should start listening to:

Dr. Moshe Milevsky—BA in mathematics and physics, MA in mathematics and statistics, PhD in business finance from York University, and professor of finance at the Schulich School of Business at York University
MosheMilevsky.com

Ed Slott—CPA, nationally recognized IRA expert, and author who has appeared on several PBS public television specials
IRAhelp.com

Tom Hegna—Retirement planning expert, highly sought-after industry speaker, economist, and best-selling author
TomHegna.com

Dr. David Babbel—BA in economics, PhD in finance from the University of Florida, and professor emeritus at the Wharton School of the University of Pennsylvania
CRAI.com/expert/david-f-babbel

Dr. Craig B. Merrill—BA in economics from Brigham Young University, PhD in insurance and finance from the University of Pennsylvania, and professor at the Marriott School of Brigham Young University
Marriottschool.byu.edu/directory/details?id=2756

Dr. Wade Pfau—Chartered Financial Analyst (CFA), PhD in economics from Princeton, and professor at the American College of Financial Services
Retirementresearcher.com

All of them have done extensive independent, real-world research. I follow them because they follow the math and facts, and you will be better off doing so too.

I hope this first chapter has helped to open your eyes and see these misconceptions for what they actually are—especially regarding Wall Street, the big brand-name and discount brokerage firms, and the media pundits' advice. If so, then you're prepared to appreciate and embrace the rest of the ideas and strategies discussed in this book. Here we go!

----

1   http://www.investinganswers.com/education/how-invest/cagr-vs-average-annual-return-why-your-advisor-quoting-wrong-number-1996

2   http://www.moneychimp.com/features/market_cagr.htm

3   http://www.moneychimp.com/features/market_cagr.htm

4   http://www.moneychimp.com/features/market_cagr.htm

5   Morningstar provides data and research insights on a wide range of investment offerings, including managed investment products, publicly listed companies, private capital markets, and real-time global market data.

6   In Chapter 7, you will learn why *pre-tax* contributions may not be the most prudent strategy for your retirement.

7   Stable value funds are capital preservation investment options available in 401(k) plans and other types of savings plans. They are invested in a high quality, diversified fixed income portfolio that are protected against interest rate volatility by contracts from banks and insurance companies. Stable value funds are designed to preserve capital while providing steady, positive returns. Stable value funds are considered a conservative and low risk investment compared to other investments offered in 401(k) plans.

8   Have your financial advisor explain, even if perhaps not applicable, in what circumstances you would *not* want to roll over your 401(k) into an IRA. Remember, it's about having knowledge.

9   There are exceptions in the tax code, as of the writing of this book, where income taxes are not due when certain qualified charities are named as the beneficiary. However, just like anything within the tax code, this can change at any time.

10   Bankrate.com

11   A prospectus is a formal legal document that is required by and filed with the Securities and Exchange Commission that provides details about an investment offering for sale to the public.

12   http://www.moneychimp.com/features/market_cagr.htm

13   Municipal bond issuers must pay an insurance premium to obtain insurance coverage for their bonds. Although investors do not pay these premiums directly, the fact that issuers and investment firms pay them means that these costs get transferred to investors. These costs are passed on in the form of lower interest rates on insured bonds.

14   Vanguard Study: https://www.vanguard.com/pdf/ISGQVAA.pdf

15   Jeff Titak, "Jeff Titak LinkedIn Profile," LinkedIn.com, accessed 1/22/2018, https://www.linkedIn.com/in/jefftitak/locale=de DE_

16   https://www.daveramsey.com/askdave/investing/finding-12

[17] https://www.daveramsey.com/blog/how-to-wreck-your-nest-egg-at-retirement

[18] https://www.nytimes.com/2007/02/25/magazine/25wwlnq4.t.html

[19] http://www.moneychimp.com/features/market_cagr.htm

[20] https://www.crestmontresearch.com

CHAPTER 2

The Risk of Sequence of Investment Returns and the Impact of Market Volatility

Sequence of investment returns involves the order in which the positive and negative investment returns occur. Let me pose a question: During the accumulation phase, does it matter when the positive and negative returns occur? What would be your assumption? Most people would probably assume that it doesn't matter. Perhaps some have no idea. That's certainly been my experience when asking people.

Let's take a look. Assume you have $1 million invested. If your investment had annual returns in the following sequence: +10 percent, –10 percent, +10 percent, –10 percent, what would be the value of your investment after four years? How about if your investment had the opposite sequence of returns each year instead: –10 percent, +10 percent, –10 percent, +10 percent? What would be the value of your investment after four years in this scenario? Let's look at the results.

$1 Million initial investment

	Scenario 1	Scenario 2
Year 1	+10%	–10%
Year 2	–10%	+10%
Year 3	+10%	–10%
Year 4	–10%	+10%
Ending value	$980,100	$980,100

If you had said the investment values would be the same, you would've been correct. The value in each scenario would be $980,100. It didn't matter that each year's returns occurred in opposite order. This confirms that while you are accumulating money (i.e., the accumulation phase, which will be explained further in Chapter 4), the sequence or timing of your investment returns is usually not that important. However, it's very important to note that it *would* make a difference if you reacted like many investors usually do by selling when the market is down and then buying after it's back up. This is quite common behavior among many investors. Former heavyweight boxing champion Mike Tyson once said, "Everyone has a plan till they get punched in the mouth." The same can be said for many investors. They have a plan until the markets drop and they look at their investment statements. For many, that's worse than a punch in the mouth. It's quite easy to set up a plan that looks great on paper. However, all it takes is an unexpected event to occur to throw your plan (and your confidence) off. That's when most people end up making emotional and ill-advised financial decisions.

Now, what if you are retired and taking distributions for income (i.e., cash flow)? Does the sequence of investment returns change the outcome? Let's take a look.

Let's assume you have $1 million invested, but you're now retired and withdrawing $50,000 each year (5 percent of the initial value). Scenario 3 (illustrated below) assumes you gain 10 percent each of the first two years, then lose 10 percent each of the next two years. Scenario 4 assumes the exact opposite—you lose 10 percent each of the first two years, then gain 10 percent each of the next two years.

Would you still have the same account value after year 4 in scenarios 3 and 4, as did the comparison of the accumulation years in scenarios 1 and 2 that had no retirement withdrawals for income? Did it change the outcome? Absolutely! In scenario 3, your account value would be $801,040, and in scenario 4 your account value would be $761,145. A difference of almost $40,000.

$1 Million initial investment with a
5 percent annual withdrawal rate (cash flow of $50,000/year)

	Scenario 3	Scenario 4
Year 1	+10%	−10%
Year 2	+10%	−10%
Year 3	−10%	+10%
Year 4	−10%	+10%
Ending value	$801,040	$761,145

You now have a potential problem that you may not even realize, at least not yet. That's because, the question now becomes, "Can you continue to withdrawal $50,000 a year for retirement income (i.e., cash flow) based on these reduced account values and not run the risk of depleting your account to zero?" Remember, if there is no account value, there is no income or cash flow. For example, in scenario 4, you would no longer be withdrawing income at a 5 percent withdrawal rate. That's because the value is no longer $1 million; it's now $761,145. Withdrawing $50,000 based on that value would be at an approximate 6.6 percent withdrawal rate. How sustainable do you think that is?

Of course, you could reduce the amount that you are withdrawing each year going forward. But could you realistically do that? Would you even want to put yourself in such a position in the first place? And remember, we haven't even considered what might happen in year 5? What if the markets continue to decline and your account continues to lose value along with another year of withdrawals for income? If you decided the prudent or safe decision, based on the current investment value of your account in scenario 4 ($761,145), was to lower your withdrawal amount to 5 percent of $761,145, then your newly adjusted annual income would provide you with only $38,057. That's almost 24 percent *less* income (cash flow). Of course, the other option is to continue withdrawing $50,000 but then you increase the risk of running out of money.

Here is another hypothetical example starting with a $1 million initial investment at an initial 5 percent withdrawal rate and increases at 3.5 percent each year:

Year	Rate of Return	Withdrawal Amount	Investment Balance
1	–15%	$50,000.00	$800,000
2	7%	$51,750.00	$804,250
3	9%	$53,561.25	$823,071
4	27%	$55,435.89	$989,865
5	–15%	$57,376.15	$784,009
6	7%	$59,384.32	$779,505
7	9%	$61,462.77	$788,198
8	27%	$63,613.96	$937,397
9	–15%	$65,840.45	$730,947
10	7%	$68,144.87	$713,969
11	9%	$70,529.94	$707,696
12	27%	$72,998.49	$825,775
13	–15%	$75,553.43	$626,355
14	7%	$78,197.80	$592,003
15	9%	$80,934.73	$564,348
16	27%	$83,767.44	$632,955
17	–15%	$86,699.30	$451,312
18	7%	$89,733.78	$393,170
19	9%	$92,874.46	$335,681
20	27%	$96,125.07	$330,189

Year	Rate of Return	Withdrawal Amount	Investment Balance
21	−15%	$99,489.44	$181,172
22	7%	$102,971.57	$90,882
23	9%	$99,061.80	$0

The outcome is that your account was depleted in year 23. As a result, you would no longer receive any retirement income or cash flow from that account. If you started this in your 60s, there's a good chance you'd still be alive and now must figure out how to replace that income in your mid 80s. Not a good position to be in, right?

Oh, and by the way, all the while, as your account was dwindling in this scenario, the *average rate of return* was a positive 6 percent per year. Just another example that you can't rely on average rates of return.

Market Volatility

We all know that the stock market and individual stock prices fluctuate (i.e., go up and down). The fluctuations in the market can be subtle, moderate, and sometimes extreme. This is referred to as market volatility. Low volatility simply means minor fluctuations in the stock market or stock prices, and high volatility means greater fluctuations in the stock market or stock prices. (Bond prices can fluctuate also, but usually not to the same degree as stocks.)

We often hear that market volatility can be good. The rationale is that when stock prices, or the market as a whole, are down, you have the opportunity to buy shares at lower prices, and assuming you have a long-term time horizon, the value of those shares are likely to eventually go back up. Therefore, market volatility does not really matter in the long-term. However, the independent research on market volatility suggests less volatility is better for the long-term growth of your investments. Here is what Roger G. Ibbotson, PhD, MBA, and Daniel Kim, PhD, MBA (*Risk and Return Within the Stock Market: What Works Best?* 2017) have concluded regarding their independent research on the topic of market volatility: "Contrary to the conventional wisdom on risk and reward, most portfolio sorting metrics exhibit an inverse risk-return relationship, with lower risk portfolios outperforming higher risk portfolios. A broad theme that emerges from the empirical evidence is that popularity underperforms." The research further states, "Contrary to theory, low beta[1] and low volatility portfolios outperform high beta and high volatility portfolios."

Also, always consider the source. Those who try and influence you into believing that volatility is not a concern likely have a vested interest in you investing your money in the stock market. They will always try to rationalize and even understate the risks.

The Impact of Market Volatility

Let's look at some investment examples to help illustrate the impact of market volatility. They each assume an initial one-time investment of $100,000 for a 4-year period. For example, in Investment 1 below, the assumption is your Year 1 rate of return (on the $100,000) was +10 percent, Year 2 –10 percent, Year 3 +10 percent, and finally, Year 4 –10 percent.

Investment 1

Year 1	+10%
Year 2	–10%
Year 3	+10%
Year 4	–10%

Your initial investment of $100,000 is now $98,010. Your average rate of return is zero, however, you *lost* money. (You learned the reason for this in Chapter 1's misconception: The average rate of return is an accurate gauge of your investment performance.)

Investment 2

Year 1	+5%
Year 2	–5%
Year 3	+5%
Year 4	–5%

Your initial investment of $100,000 is now $99,500. Your average rate of return is also zero, but you have $1,490 *more money* than in Investment 1. The reason for this is that Investment 2 was less volatile than Investment 1. You may not have earned as much on the upside but, more importantly, you didn't lose as much on the downside. Thus, you earned more money.

Investment 3

Year 1	+20%
Year 2	–10%
Year 3	+20%
Year 4	–10%

Your investment of $100,000 is now $116,640. Your average rate of return is 5 percent.

Investment 4

Year 1	+5%
Year 2	+5%
Year 3	+5%
Year 4	+5%

Your investment of $100,000 is now $121,550. You have the same average rate of return (5 percent) as Investment 3, but you have gained $4,910 more than Investment 3. Again, that's because Investment 4 was not just less volatile compared to Investment 3, it had no volatility and no losses.

Now, let's look at Investment 5 to see an example of how fast you can lose what you have accumulated.

Investment 5

Year 1	+17.35%
Year 2	+17.70%
Year 3	+3.12%
Year 4	+8.67%
Year 5	+22.96%

The average rate of return is 13.96 percent. Now, let's add in an additional year, which included a huge market drop (like in 2008):

Year 1	+17.35%
Year 2	+17.70%
Year 3	+3.12%
Year 4	+8.67%
Year 5	+22.96%
Year 6	−44.14%

Now the average rate of return is only 4.27 percent—more than a 9 percentage point difference.

Put in terms of actual dollars (excluding taxes and fees), if you invested $100,000, in five-years, your investment would have grown to $190,000. However, by being invested for an additional year that included a large market drop, your initial $100,000 investment that grew to $190,000 dropped all the way down to $106,000. What a difference one-year can make!

This next example assumes you are investing $12,000 a year into your retirement account and you earn 9 percent a year. In 25 years, your retirement account value is $1,107,887[2] (not adjusting for fees or taxes). You contributed a total of $300,000 toward your retirement ($12,000 multiplied by 25 [years] equals $300,000). Your earnings were $807,887—this is the difference between the account value in 25 years and the total contributions made to the account. That's very good. With more than $1 million, you might think you can now retire. However, right before you retire, or the first year that you retired, there is a huge market crash like we had in 2008, and your retirement account loses 30 percent of its value. It is now valued at only $775,520—a loss of more than $300,000. Put in more depressing terms, that's the $300,000 (and more) you contributed of your hard-earned money toward your retirement account for those 25 years! In just one year, you lost every dollar that you invested for all those years toward your retirement. This may seem like an extreme example to some, but is it? It certainly isn't when you consider times such as what happened in the stock market from 2000-02 and in 2008. Remember, market volatility and market corrections are very difficult to predict. They can happen at any time. And millions of people learned this the hard way during the past two severe market corrections. The lesson is that it can take you many years (and sacrifices) to accumulate a substantial amount of money and, in a very short period of time, much of it can be lost. Don't allow yourself to be put in such a situation.

Now let's look at market volatility as it relates to both average and real rates of return[3] using the S&P 500® index as an example. From 1990 through 1999, the index had an average rate of return of 19.11 percent and a real rate of return of 18.30 percent. Not much difference as result of mostly strong positive years in the stock market with only one modestly negative year. Now, let's factor in the three negative years that followed (2000-02). The average rate of return from 1990–2002 dropped to 11.36 percent and the real rate of return (that adjusts for volatility and losses) dropped to just 9.72 percent. There is certainly a difference once those negative years are factored in.

From 2000 through 2015, the average rate of return of the S&P 500® index was 5.78 percent. The real rate of return was only 4.02 percent. (Imagine if you had used the Dave Ramsey or Suze Orman high rates of return projections during this time period? Or, how about if you had used their high withdrawal rate assumptions as well?)

From 2003 through 2007 (after the stock market plummeted in 2000–2002, but prior to the market crash in 2008), the average rate of return was 13.11 percent with a real rate of return of 12.78 percent. Again, there wasn't much of a difference between the two because the stock market was up during this period and there were no negative years. Now let's include the following year, 2008, when the S&P 500® dropped more than 37 percent. The average rate of return from 2003 through 2008 dropped from 13.11 percent to 4.72 percent and the real rate of return dropped even further to just 2.29 percent.

Therein lies the problem and the *real* risk investors face when subject to market volatility and losses. All it takes is *one* bad year to erase most or even all the gains you had previously accumulated. As you have seen, the more volatile the markets and your investment portfolio are, the more your money is at risk and also subject to a reduced real rate of return, which results in accumulating a lot less money.

Are Equal Gains and Losses a Wash?

Many people may naively assume that if their investment account gained and then lost the same percentage (e.g., gained 10 percent, then lost 10 percent), their investment account value would be back to even. This isn't the case. For example, let's say your initial investment is $10,000 and your investment account grows 10 percent the first year, meaning its value is now $11,000, excluding fees and taxes for illustrative purposes. Next year, your investment account declines 10 percent. Are you back to $10,000? Many people may think so. Up 10 percent, down 10 percent is a wash, right? However, that would be incorrect. Remember, the loss in your investment account was based off its current value of $11,000, not your initial investment of $10,000. Thus, a 10 percent loss equals $1,100—reducing your investment account to $9,900. The next question is: What rate of return is required to get your investment account back to $11,000? Since you're catching on now, you know it's not 10 percent. It's actually 11.12 percent.

Let's now assume a 20 percent gain followed by a 20 percent loss on the same initial $10,000 investment. The investment account would be $12,000 after the first year, and the next year it would drop to $9,600. Now, what rate of return is required to get back to the $12,000 value? Again, not the same 20 percent, but rather 25 percent.

A Simple Look at the Math

You've now seen that percentage *gains* need to be higher than percentage *losses* just to get back to even, or to where the prior account value was. For the sake of clarity, the table below illustrates what the percentage gains need to be after losses to get back to even. Note that the bigger the percentage loss, the percentage gain needed to get back to even is exponentially greater.

Investment loss	Rate of return to get back to even
–5%	+5.3%
–10%	+11.1%
–20%	+25%
–30%	+42.9%
–40%	+66.7%
–50%	+100%

Remember, this is just to get back to even. Now let's look at the percentage gain needed the following year to "get back on track" as if the account had continued to grow and never lost value and assuming the investment was growing at 6 percent.

Investment loss	Rate of return needed to catch back up rather than *just* get back to even
–10%	+24.8%
–20%	+40.5%
–30%	+60.5%
–40%	+87.3%
–50%	+124.7%

Remember, the investment could still lose value, rather than gain value, the following year and therefore would require an even higher rate of return to get back on track.

Low-Correlation or Noncorrelation versus Diversification

Let's first discuss diversification. The objective of diversification is to help lessen the potential risk in your portfolio by not putting all your eggs into one basket. For example, instead of buying two or three individual stocks, you invest in a mutual fund that may consist of hundreds of stocks.

Another example of diversification is to create an investment portfolio consisting of different asset classes. This may consist of a combination of large cap stocks, small cap stocks, international stocks, real estate stocks, etc. It can also include bonds. Creating an investment portfolio with these asset classes would be considered diversified by most industry standards.

However, diversification still puts your investment portfolio at risk due to market volatility. This is especially true if they are all highly correlated as most stock market investment portfolios are.

Let's take a look at how diversification failed during the market collapse of 2008 by looking at the following traditional market indices.[4]

- S&P 500   −37.00%
- MSCI EAFE   −43.06%
- S&P US Real Estate   −39.20%
- Lipper Balanced   −26.19%
- MSCI Emerging Mkts   −53.20%

As you can clearly see, by looking at the above negative index returns for these asset classes, diversification failed, and failed miserably in 2008.

Now, let's look at the following year: 2009.

- S&P 500   +26.46%
- MSCI EAFE   +32.46%
- S&P US Real Estate   +28.46%
- Lipper Balanced   +23.36%
- MSCI Emerging Mkts   +79.02%

As you can also see, these traditional asset classes are highly correlated with each other. This is why they all dropped in 2008 and then all went up in 2009. It doesn't always happen this way, but clearly it can, because it has. Diversification has its benefits, but it's not the ideal risk-management strategy to try to temper market volatility. Managing risk solely through diversification is not a prudent strategy.

What Makes Low-Correlation or Noncorrelation Different from Diversification?

Now let's look at what correlation is and how low-correlation or noncorrelation to the markets can help to temper the volatility of the investment portfolio as a whole.

Asset correlation is a measure of how investments move in relation to one another and when. When assets move in the same direction at the same time, they are considered to be highly correlated. When one asset tends to move up while another goes down, the two assets are considered to be less or noncorrelated. It's that simple.

In contrast to diversification, low- or noncorrelation means your assets are less likely to be impacted by market volatility, certainly less than if your investments were highly correlated. It doesn't necessarily mean you won't lose value or you will get better returns. That's not what I am implying. The main objective is to potentially help minimize the volatility of your overall portfolio due to the highly correlated investments that you likely already have in your portfolio (i.e., lessen the ups and downs, or fluctuations, in your investment portfolio). There are many ways to add low- and noncorrelated assets to your portfolio, for example, commodities such as gold, emerging market bonds, non-traded real estate investment trusts, private equity, fixed annuities, and cash value life insurance. This strategy will be explored further in Chapter 3. This is also where you will definitely want to talk with a trusted, independent, and experienced financial advisor!

When Should You Address the Risk of Market Volatility?

Market volatility should be discussed, and dealt with, at the time you *set up* your investment portfolio and not while you are actually experiencing volatility of your investments. This planning can help you potentially eliminate the surprises (and there are always surprises) and help you react rationally rather than emotionally.

An emotional investor can be the most detrimental type. Many people think they are more risk-tolerant than they actually are, and they often have an investment portfolio they think is risk averse and has low volatility when it actually is not. With my clients, I not only try to fully understand their perception of risk but also help educate them of the risks associated with market volatility. I feel it's very important to point out to them the impact it can potentially have before it occurs.

Remember, protecting the downside of your investments is much more important than trying to grow your investments by taking more risk. As you have seen, losing principal sets your investment back and hinders the ability for continued growth. As a result, you must first wait for the investment to recover (i.e., regain the value prior to the loss) before you can potentially obtain any actual gain or growth. And, who's to say the investment won't decline over an extended period of time (e.g., a bear market)? The fact is, the negative returns have a greater impact on your investments than the positive returns, even if the average rates of return are the same. Slow and steady is a better investment strategy—be the tortoise, not the hare, when it comes to your investment strategy. Adding low- or noncorrelated assets to your portfolio can help accomplish this.

Market volatility can have even worse consequences when you are taking withdrawals in retirement. Therefore, don't let market volatility hinder your retirement income (i.e., cash flow) strategy either.

Finally, there is a great white paper on the impact of volatility called "Math Matters: Rethinking Investment Returns and How Math Impacts Results," provided by Swan Global Investments. I strongly suggest you read it. You can access it through their website at SwanGlobalInvestments.com/math-matters-rethinking-investment-returns or through my Mappa Wealth Management website at mappawm.com under the links tab.

———————

[1] Beta is a measure used in fundamental analysis to determine the volatility of an asset or portfolio in relation to the overall market.

[2] Bankrate.com

[3] Moneychimp.com

[4] Symmetry Partners:

S&P 500 Index is an unmanaged group of securities considered to be representative of the stock market in general.

The Lipper Balanced Fund Index of mutual funds is unmanaged and includes the 30 largest funds within the Lipper Balanced Fund investment category. This Index does not include the effect of expenses and cannot be invested in directly.

S&P United States REIT Index measures the investable universe of publicly traded real estate investment trusts.

The MSCI EAFE Index (Europe, Australasia, Far East) is a free-float-adjusted market capitalization index that is designed to measure the equity market performance of developed markets, excluding the United States and Canada. The MSCI EAFE Index consists of the following 22 developed market country indices: Australia, Austria, Belgium, Denmark, Finland, France, Germany, Greece, Hong Kong, Ireland, Israel, Italy, Japan, the Netherlands, New Zealand, Norway, Portugal, Singapore, Spain, Sweden, Switzerland, and the United Kingdom.

The MSCI Emerging Markets Index is a free-float-adjusted market capitalization index that is designed to measure equity market performance of emerging markets. The MSCI Emerging Markets Index consists of the following 21 emerging market country indices: Brazil, Chile, China, Colombia, Czech Republic, Egypt, Hungary, India, Indonesia, Korea, Malaysia, Mexico, Morocco, Peru, Philippines, Poland, Russia, South Africa, Taiwan, Thailand, and Turkey.

Investing internationally carries additional risks such as differences in financial reporting, currency exchange risk, as well as economic and political risk unique to the specific country. Investments in emerging markets may be more volatile and less liquid than investing in developed markets and may involve exposure to economic structures that are generally less diverse and mature and to political systems that have less stability than those of more developed countries.

CHAPTER 3

How the Wealthy Save and Invest, and Why You Should Follow Their Philosophy

I'm always saying, "Save and invest like the wealthy." However, it's important to know that you definitely don't have to be wealthy to save and invest the same way they do. It's the principles and strategies the wealthy use that you can also apply, regardless of net worth, that matters. It is also how the wealthy *think* about money and that you should learn to think the same way. Remember, how you think is everything, as it determines your behavior. The wealthy also save and invest their money much differently from how we have been taught by Wall Street, the big brand-name and discount brokerage firms, and media pundits. It's important to note that just because someone is wealthy doesn't mean they have a higher tolerance for risk, don't care if they lose money, or are less concerned about fees. It's quite the contrary.

Let's take a look. The wealthy think in terms of return *of* their money (i.e., protecting their principal and getting their principal back) whereas most of us are taught to think in terms of return *on* our money (i.e., the rates of return we can get). The wealthy think in terms of getting *value* for their money whereas most of us are taught to think in terms of lowest cost or cheaper is better. (The misconception that cheaper is better was addressed in Chapter 1.) For example, the wealthy wouldn't balk at paying a fee of say 2 or 3 percent on an investment opportunity if that investment had the potential for a 9 or 10 (or higher) percent net return or yield (i.e., cash flow) after the fees were deducted. However, the rest of us have been led to believe that we would be far better off to focus primarily on the fees and therefore solely seek out investments that charge the lowest fees possible (as promoted by Schwab, Fidelity, Vanguard, etc.) even if that resulted in a lower net return or incurred more market risk. Exploring this further, let's say someone is paying a fee of 0.5 percent on an investment with a historical or potential 5–7 percent return or yield (i.e., cash flow) *before* any fees are deducted. They will happily accept that because they're only paying a half-percent fee. They would likely not even consider an investment that charges a fee of say 1 or 2 percent but has a higher (or even similar) historical or potential net return such as 6-8 percent *after* the 1 or 2 percent in fees and with less risk due to lower market volatility. Think about that, the latter investment has a historical or potential higher net rate of return *after* fees and accomplished this with less risk yet it's still perceived as too expense by the average investor. Does this even make any sense? Of course, it doesn't! What matters most is what you actually *keep* after fees and taxes, not *just* the fees. Plus, you have to consider any benefits or unique features provided. You should learn to think the same way too. Remember, don't be penny wise and dollar foolish.

Have you ever watched the TV show *Shark Tank*? Aside from its entertainment value, you should watch it so you can understand how these wealthy investors (the "Sharks") think about money. For example, you'll never hear them talk about the rate of return they "hope" to get. Or what the costs or fees are... ever. What you hear them repeatedly ask the entrepreneurs, who are seeking an investment from the Sharks, is how will they get their money back (i.e., return of their money) and how the business they are considering investing in will provide cash flow. Cash flow from these investments is a huge part of what helps them to earn a high rate of return in the first place. In fact, you often hear them offering deals that include licensing agreements[1] or royalties.[2] In addition, they sometimes offer to provide a loan as part of the deal. They favor these options because it provides an ongoing stream of cash flow. They prefer to be earning something on their investment while they are waiting for the return of their money. It's also how they get their money (i.e., investment) back so that they can then seek out other investment opportunities. As I've repeatedly said, cash flow is what you need to focus on, not rates of return. The Sharks and the wealthy certainly understand this. In fact, one of the show's Sharks is longtime investor Kevin O'Leary, and here is what he has to say on the subject:

> "What you learn as an investor over multiple decades
> is the only thing that matters is free cash flow. That's it."
> from the book *Kevin O'Leary: Shark's INVESTING Rules*

The wealthy also take calculated risk when making an investment. Calculated risk means having the knowledge to understand what factors need to occur, along with the expectations that they will, in order for an investment to be profitable. It also means being aware of the potential things that could go wrong or what could adversely affect the investment opportunity (e.g., changes in interest rates on an investment that involves debt or currency risk on an investment outside the United States). In some circumstances, the potential risks can be mitigated or hedged. For example, using options[3] or futures[4] or perhaps adding noncorrelated or nontraded assets. I'm mentioning these strategies for your awareness but keep in mind that they're best to outsource to a professional, unless of course, you are trained or already an expert in one of these areas, for example, your profession is an options trader. That's because doing it wrong can result in the exact opposite of what you intended—reducing risk. You don't want to magnify your risk or loss when you are trying to minimize it. An independent financial advisor can help you find what's most appropriate.

Most people, however, aren't doing any of this or even thinking about it. Instead of taking any sort of calculated risk, they are putting their money into the stock market and then *hoping* the markets go up. If they want any "protection" to reduce risk, they add bonds (which really isn't protection). The truth is, most people don't even know what makes the markets go up or down, and yet they invest in it anyway because "everyone else" is doing it. Their investment strategy isn't calculated, it is in the form of hope. This doesn't sound like a very prudent investment strategy, does it?

The wealthy also look to take advantage of investment opportunities that come around from time to time, such as a potentially lucrative business opportunity to invest in. They also seek to take advantage of investment opportunities that are fundamentally sound but perhaps are currently out of favor, or ones that have lost value due to the emotions of average investors who are in sell mode. For example, this could mean buying stocks or real estate after the values have plummeted—or investing in oil, natural gas, or some other commodity when prices have dropped substantially due to economic, market, or political factors.

Here is a specific example of taking advantage of investment opportunities. In the mid-2000s when so many people were buying and investing in real estate as the supposed next "can't lose" opportunity. However, rapid price increases eventually led to unsustainable real estate valuations creating a bubble. The wealthy, however, had the patience to wait and not buy simply because everyone else was doing so (remember what Warren Buffett said in Chapter 1). Once that bubble burst, which was inevitable, the values plummeted and there was plenty of opportunity if you had the resources (i.e., available and accessible cash) to start buying and investing.

Here is another example. During this same time period (mid-2000s), the stock market was recovering from the recession and market meltdown. The average investor was now feeling very comfortable not only investing but investing more aggressively in the stock market. However, just like with real estate at that time, risk was increasing as values continued to rise beyond rational levels. Then in 2008, like real estate, the stock market crashed and investors were now thinking there was too much risk and staying invested only meant they would lose even more.

This way of thinking happens all too often and is exactly how the average investor thinks. However, this is certainly not how the wealthy think; they see it as an opportunity, and better yet, the wealthy make certain that they are prepared to take advantage of those investment opportunities by having money available and accessible. You certainly won't have money available or accessible if it's all tied up in the stock market or your 401(k).

Mark Cuban, businessman, investor, owner of the Dallas Mavericks, and a regular on the TV show *Shark Tank,* recently said, "Invest when there's blood in the streets." He then added, "I would rather have a lot of cash on hand for that time when things go bad." (CNBC.com)

Let's summarize by analyzing what one of the greatest and wealthiest investors, Warren Buffett did. In 2011, in the middle of the Great Recession, he provided a financial "lifeline" to Bank of America by investing $5 billion dollars in the company. This investment gave him, via his company Berkshire Hathaway, shares of preferred stock in Bank of America that provided a 6 percent yield as well as warrants[5] with the right to convert these warrants to shares of common stock in Bank of America at a future date. In 2017, he exercised these warrants. This tripled his initial investment and resulted in a profit of approximately $12 billion dollars in just six years.[6] Lucky him, right? Or was it luck? Let's break down the seven steps Buffett took, and that the wealthy consistently utilize.

1. Seeking and recognizing opportunity

Warren Buffett saw an opportunity to make an investment that offered a great deal of upside potential. This was a time when the average investor only saw risk and continued losses.

2. Seeking value

Buffett wasn't looking at this opportunity and thinking, *what will it cost?* Sure, there were fees and expenses to make this opportunity happen. However, his focus was on whether or not this investment provided value and the potential for gain in lieu of the cost or fees.

3. Availability and accessibility to cash

Buffett is always looking for investment opportunities to take advantage of. That's what has made him so successful as an investor. In order to be prepared for these opportunities, he maintains readily available access to cash. This allowed him to quickly seize the opportunity to invest in Bank of America.

4. Calculated risk

He didn't just hope the investment would be a solid one. He understood the risk involved, the potential gain, and what needed to actually occur to make this a prudent investment.

5. Not following the crowd

This was certainly a time when the average investor was extremely skittish about putting money in the stock market—in fact, they were taking their money out. Not Warren Buffett. As he has been quoted saying, "Be fearful when others are greedy, and be greedy when others are fearful!"

6. Cash Flow

While he was waiting for the return of his money (followed by a return on his money), he was getting compensated with a rather healthy cash flow from the preferred stock dividend.

7. Patience

He wasn't in any hurry for his money back, nor did he expect to see high returns on his investment quickly, as so many other investors tend to do. His initial plan was to exercise the warrants sometime in the year 2021. So even though they were exercised just six years later, his original time horizon was long term.

Don't be Afraid of the "L" Word or the "B" Word

"L" is for leverage and "B" is for borrowing. The wealthy understand the benefits of prudent leveraging and borrowing. However, we hear from so many of the media pundits, like Suze Orman and Dave Ramsey, who say that *all debt* is bad and you should pay off all your debt as soon as possible, before you do anything else. The reality is that not *all* debt is bad. As I discussed in Chapter 1, you also have to consider opportunity cost. For example, if you can borrow money at 3 percent and invest it for a potential 7 percent rate of return (or cash flow rate) then this is something you very well may want to consider. And of course, real estate has historically been a very popular and prudent way to take advantage of financial leverage. Most successful real estate investors understand this and use leverage to their advantage. Borrowing and using leverage can be an even more attractive option when interest rates are low.

Where the Wealthy Put Their Money

The following[7] are just some of the places where the wealthy often put their money:

- Real estate
- Private equity
- Private debt
- Dividend-paying stocks and mutual funds
- Annuities
- High cash value life insurance
- Commodities, managed futures, options and hedging strategies (generally as risk management strategies)

These savings and investments are used because they can potentially provide many of the key features and benefits I have been discussing. These include low-correlation to the stock market, lower volatility, potential tax benefits, and most important, many of these savings and investments provide cash flow. Aside from high cash value life insurance and fixed annuities, these are at-risk investments, meaning your principal can lose value, just like stocks, bonds, mutual funds, etc. can lose value. Some of these investments are illiquid, meaning they cannot be converted to cash quickly and/or easily. However, it's very important to note that this lack of liquidity is what actually helps to make these investments less correlated and even less volatile compared to the stock and bond markets. This is why I say that liquidity is not an investor's friend. The truth is, if you need liquidity, you probably shouldn't be invested in at-risk investments in the first place. Why put your money at risk when you may be needing it in the near future? It doesn't make any sense. I also believe that if you're investing for the long term, such as for retirement, you really don't need liquidity either. What's the point? You aren't going to be using those retirement dollars until many years or decades from now. Furthermore, because liquid at-risk investments are usually highly correlated to the stock and bond markets it can result in higher volatility, and you have already seen how that can negatively impact your investment portfolio.

Remember, the wealthy are far less concerned with liquidity and far more focused on making their money work for them as efficiently as possible while also prudently protecting against loss. They are therefore typically very patient investors. Conversely, the average investor is usually very impatient and far too concerned with liquidity and rates of return. Furthermore, the wealthy don't place most of their money in the stock market, as we are taught to do from Wall Street, the big brand-name and discount brokerage firms, and media pundits. The money that they do put into stocks or in the stock market is usually directed toward low volatility and low-correlated investment strategies that also can provide cash flow. That's how they get the best use and value of their invested money.

I strongly encourage you to discuss these saving and investment opportunities with an independent financial advisor to see which of them are appropriate for you. Then look to fit them into your financial plan.

High Cash Value Life Insurance—"Do as Wall Street Does, Not as They Say"

We have been taught by Wall Street, the big brand-name and discount brokerage firms, and by many of the media pundits that life insurance should only be purchased for the death benefit and never for cash accumulation, whether for saving or investing. They also tell us that cash value life insurance is not a good investment and that there are other more appropriate places for your cash accumulation objectives. And, when there is a need for life insurance, they preach buying only term life insurance and investing the difference. In fact, that's their mantra: "Buy term and invest the difference."

However, if you look into this more closely, you'll see that Wall Street banks buy large amounts of cash value life insurance. In fact, here is a short list of some of the biggest banks that own cash value life insurance along with the current cash value of that insurance:

Bank of America $19,607,000,000
Wells Fargo Bank $17,739,000,000
JP Morgan Chase $10,327,000,000
U.S. Bank $5,451,892,000

Yes, that's *billions* of dollars each bank has in cash value life insurance! According to FDIC.gov, as of 2017, banks own more than $160 billion in cash value life insurance.

Why is that? What aren't they telling us? Remember, these are the same Wall Street bankers telling us how *horrible* cash value life insurance is.

It's important to understand that just because something is used or was created for one purpose doesn't mean it can't have other uses or purposes. For example, did you know there are many drugs that were developed for one particular medical issue, yet they are actually prescribed by doctors for other, completely different, medical issues? Botox is a perfect example. Botox was initially used to treat muscle spasms and eventually other medically related symptoms. But now it is commonly used for nonsurgical cosmetic procedures. There are many examples like this. The point is, just because something was initially developed for one thing, doesn't mean it can't be put to use for a different or more appropriate purpose. It all goes back to how you think.

Cash value life insurance is another example because it, too, can have many uses. Of course, first and foremost, it provides a death benefit. In fact, using cash value life insurance to leave money to beneficiaries or for estate-planning purposes is a great idea and a very prudent strategy. However, it can also be a prudent cash accumulation vehicle. That's because the cash value of the life insurance policy can be used in many instances such as to provide cash needs in the event of a financial emergency, to provide a loan to make a purchase, to access cash for an investment opportunity, or to provide tax-free cash flow for retirement. In fact, that is exactly how many people used cash value life insurance decades ago.

Let's look at the facts. For one, the cash value of most life insurance policies is *not* meant for investing (the one exception being variable universal life). They are not investments and therefore shouldn't be categorized as such nor compared to them; it's like comparing apples-to-oranges. They were designed to be (and in most cases, still are) a savings vehicle. That being said, now is a good time to define the difference between savings and investments—an important distinction absolutely worth understanding. Savings is for your "safe" money that incurs little or no principal risk. It can be for your short-term, medium-term, and even your long-term financial objectives. Investments are for your "at-risk" money. It's money you can afford to lose. You should understand and accept that you can potentially lose the value of your principal, even if only temporarily, such as when the price of your stock or mutual fund drops (assuming you don't sell). The fact that investing involves risk to your principal and therefore should be used for your long-term goals. It is important to understand the difference and not confuse the two. Therefore, separate your saving and investment mindsets (i.e., how you think about each).

Back to the discussion on cash value life insurance. When I talk about cash value life insurance, I am not referring to the type of policy designed to give very little or no cash value in the first few years. This is the type of policy that benefits the insurance agents in the form of higher commissions, resulting in the policy having lower initial cash value that is available to the policy owner—you. This type of policy is what you'll typically get from an agent who works for the "Northwestern Mutuals" of the world. These agents work for the insurance company, therefore you are already being subject to a conflict of interest and a bias toward buying life insurance. In addition, they can only offer you an insurance policy from one company—the one they work for. I am also not referring to the type of cash value life insurance policy where your cash value can decline due to investment losses, such as with a variable universal life policy. (An exception may be if you truly understand and can tolerate market risk for potentially higher returns or if the policy offers a guaranteed death benefit regardless of the performance of the invested cash value. However, this type of cash value life insurance policy falls into the at-risk category which again, is not what I am referring to.)

I am specifically referring to the type of cash value life insurance policy that the wealthy utilize, which is referred to as high cash value life insurance. This is typically a dividend-paying whole life, universal life, or indexed universal life insurance policy. This also happens to be the type of policy Wall Street and many Fortune 500 companies use but only for their inner circle. The objective is to maximize the cash value of the policy right from the very beginning. This allows for a lot more of the policy's cash value to be immediately available and accessible. It also provides for faster growth of the cash value. How does this happen? With more cash value in the policy from day one, means that much more of the cash value is working for *you* (think compound interest).

This is far different from the cash value life insurance policies that the rest of us are typically presented with, which do the exact opposite. Those are the policies that provide minimal to no accessible cash value during the first few years (as I just mentioned above). Therefore, there is a lot less, or even no, cash value to access if needed or wanted. This also results in having much less cash value working to help maximize the accumulation or growth of the cash value in the policy. When a cash value policy has little or no accessible cash value in the first few years, it's because the commission to the agent is higher. Conversely, when the accessible cash value is higher in the first few years, it's because the commission to the agent is much lower. It's that straightforward. That's the trade-off. Let me be clear though, there is absolutely nothing wrong with an agent or advisor earning a commission for providing a valuable service and providing appropriate and helpful advice such as when recommending a life insurance policy. However, unfortunately there are some agents who simply sell these policies solely for the commissions. This is why you may hear negative things about cash value life insurance. But don't allow some bad apples or blatantly misguided information deter you from learning whether a high cash value life insurance policy is appropriate for you or not. After all, the wealthy, Wall Street, and corporate America buy this type of life insurance. They obviously see the benefits; you should learn to see them as well.

In addition to cash value life insurance providing available and accessible cash value and not being subject to principal risk, another reason the wealthy use cash value life insurance is that it provides both tax-deferred growth and tax-free cash flow (via withdrawals up to the premiums paid into the policy and/or policy loans). This is also why Wall Street and many Fortune 500 companies use cash value life insurance to provide retirement benefits for their top executives. Even colleges and universities use cash value life insurance for these favorable tax benefits. For example, Jim Harbaugh, the former pro football quarterback and current University of Michigan head coach, amended part of his contract with the university to include a cash value life insurance policy. According to a *Forbes* article published May 11, 2017, Harbaugh would be eligible to receive an estimated $1.4 million per year in *tax-free* retirement income via policy loans[8] starting at age 66. Furthermore, per an ESPN report[9], a source at the university explained that this is a more commonplace form of deferred compensation in the corporate world. Yes! Cash value life insurance is commonplace in the corporate world. The Wall Street world too. Unfortunately, it's not commonplace in "our" world. But, it definitely should be.

The irony is (and most people aren't even aware) that years ago cash value life insurance used to be very common and a place where people would put their money. The only reason that changed was not because better options became available or these policies didn't perform well—quite the contrary. It was because Wall Street and a number of misleading promoters of term life insurance hoodwinked the American public with their aggressive marketing into believing that taking more risk earns higher returns and that term life insurance is truly less expensive than cash value life insurance and this is the best way to achieve financial security. As you know, I addressed both of these misconceptions in Chapter 1.

It's time to *not* do what Wall Street says to do and start doing what Wall Street and the corporate world does. I haven't even begun to touch the surface on how you can prudently use high cash value life insurance within your financial plan. I have personally used it for many years and have been more than satisfied. If you would like to learn more, I have provided a number of great reading recommendations at the end of this book. In addition, feel free to contact me. I'd be happy to discuss.

Allocating Your Savings and Investments Like the Wealthy

The wealthy often allocate their wealth among liquid no-risk assets, liquid at-risk assets, and lastly illiquid at-risk assets. To pursue these principles and strategies like the wealthy, I generally suggest your assets be allocated as described below. Please note: This is simply a very general guideline, a starting point. Clearly, you can and should adjust according to your own situation.

Here is a basic example:

- One-third of your money should be allocated to liquid no-risk assets such as money markets, short-term certificates of deposit (CDs) at the bank or the credit union, short-term bonds, or high cash value life insurance. Exactly which and how much you should allocate to any of these is going to be based on your own personal situation and objectives. The goal is simply to provide liquidity in case of an emergency, for upcoming major purchases, and to be prepared for investment opportunities that become available. And they will. They always do. The question is, will you be ready and able to take advantage of the opportunity? Think of your own mini version of what Warren Buffett did in 2011.

- The next third should be allocated to liquid at-risk assets, such as stocks, long-term bonds, mutual funds, exchange-traded funds (ETFs), or unit investment trusts (UITs). Remember, I am not against investing in the stock market. I just suggest you do so prudently and with less exposure than what is generally recommended by Wall Street, the big brand-name and discount brokerage firms, and media pundits. You can invest in these almost anywhere, such as through a brokerage account or through the investment company or mutual fund sponsor. Mutual funds will likely be the only available option in your company's retirement plan (e.g., 401(k), 403(b)). An independent financial advisor can provide recommendations as well.

- Finally, one-third should be allocated to illiquid at-risk assets, such as nontraded real estate investment trusts (nontraded REITs), private debt/ equity offerings, managed futures, etc. This could also be direct ownership of real estate investment properties or providing direct private loans. (Direct private loans are typically made to real estate investors and business owners.)

As you get closer to retirement, you should also start looking into annuities and how they can fit into your retirement plan. Most annuities will fall into the il-liquid no-risk asset category due to both the minimum holding or surrender charge period and safety of principal. With regard to variable annuities, they too, can fall into this classification when a guaranteed lifetime income benefit rider is included. Variable annuities with guaranteed lifetime income benefit riders don't guarantee principal but do guarantee income (based on the claims-paying ability of the insur-er). I will provide a lot more details on annuities in upcoming chapters.

Just remember, you don't have to be wealthy to save and invest like the wealthy. However, you can certainly learn from how the wealthy save and invest rather than how Wall Street, the big brand-name and discount brokerage firms, and the media pundits want you to save and invest. In my 30-plus years as an independent financial advisor, I have found the principles and strategies that the wealthy use to be very compelling.

Finally, seek advice from an independent financial advisor who understands and embraces this school of thought.

------

[1] A licensing agreement refers to a written agreement entered into by the con-tractual owner of a property or activity giving permission to another to use that property or engage in an activity in relation to that property. The property involved in a licensing agreement can be real, personal, or intellectual. Almost always, there will be some financial consideration exchanged between the licen-sor and the licensee.

[2] A royalty is a payment made by one party (the licensee or franchisee) to another that owns a particular asset (the licensor or franchisor) for the right to ongoing use of that asset. Royalties are typically agreed upon as a percentage of gross or net revenues derived from the use of an asset or a fixed price per unit sold of an item of such, but there are also other modes and metrics of compensation. A royalty interest is the right to collect a stream of future royalty payments.

[3] Options contracts are instruments that give the holder of the instrument the right to buy or sell the underlying asset at a pre-determined price. An option can be a "call" option or a "put" option. Options are not suitable for all inves-tors. There are risks involved in any option strategy. Individuals should not en-ter into option transactions until they have read and understood the option dis-closure document titled "Characteristics and Risks of Standardized Options," which outlines the purposes and risks of option transactions. This booklet is

available at http://www.theocc.com/about/publications/character-risks.jsp.

4 A future is a contract to buy or sell the underlying asset for a specific price at a pre-determined time. If you buy a futures contract, it means that you promise to pay the price of the asset at a specified time. If you sell a future, you effectively make a promise to transfer the asset to the buyer of the future at a specified price at a particular time. Trading futures involves the risk of loss and is not suitable for all investors. Please consider carefully whether futures are appropriate for your financial situation. Only risk capital should be used when trading futures. Investors could lose more than their initial investment. Carefully consider the inherent risks of such an investment in light of your financial condition.

5 A warrant is a security that entitles the holder to buy the underlying stock of the issuing company at a fixed price, called exercise price, until the expiry date.

6 https://www.cnbc.com/2017/06/30/warren-buffett-just-made-a-quick-12-billion-on-bank-of-america.html

7 These types of investments and savings vehicles are not all inclusive and may not be appropriate for everyone. Some of these investments may require a minimum income level or liquid net worth—check with your financial advisor for details and get a prospectus and any other relevant information before making any investment. Investing in real estate and other alternative investments entails certain risks, including changes in: the economy, supply and demand, laws, tenant turnover, interest rates (including periods of high interest rates), availability of mortgage funds, operating expenses, and cost of insurance. Some real estate investments offer limited liquidity options.

8 Loans/withdrawals may reduce cash values and/or the death benefit. They may also cause the policy to lapse. Depending on the status or classification of the policy, the withdrawal may not be tax-free. Individuals should consult their financial professional.

9 http://www.espn.com/college-football/story/_/id/17332547/michigan-wolverines-jim-harbaugh-agree-increased-compensation-form-life-insurance-loan

CHAPTER 4

Accumulation Planning versus Distribution Planning

The Financial Strategies You Use to Get to Retirement
Are Very Different from Those You Should Be Using During Retirement

Think of accumulation planning and distribution planning as similar to the process of mountain climbing. It's certainly not as dangerous as mountain climbing in the physical sense; however, the process and the goals are similar. Let me explain. The climber wants to get to the top before heading back down safely. In order to accomplish this goal, the climber must establish a plan, for mountains can be a dangerous and unforgiving place without one. Also, the climber must understand the many risks involved and how to minimize them. Your best chance of a successful and safe summit is to climb with a professional guide. The whole process involves studying, training, and preparation. For the most challenging of mountains, this can and will likely take years. And yet, the climber still doesn't always reach the summit because there are variables beyond his or her control (e.g., weather).

The reality is, it could take multiple attempts. If the climber doesn't succeed the first time and survives, the goal is to learn from the journey and develop a better plan of action going forward to best position for success in the future.

When the climber does achieve the summit, it's a moment of intense satisfaction and joy! It's a huge accomplishment, to say the least—and the view is beautiful. After some brief celebration at the top, it's time to focus on getting down safely. Unlike the climb to the top, there are no second chances on the way down. The reality is, the climber either makes it down or doesn't, and most accidents on the mountain happen on the way down. The climber really has just one shot at this very important goal.

This analogy likewise applies to the accumulation and distribution phases of your retirement plan. Just as it can take many attempts to get to the top of the summit, you likely will have, and need, numerous attempts and opportunities to get yourself to your retirement "summit" during the accumulation phase. However, just like climbing down the mountain, you really have just one shot at getting yourself through retirement securely. The strategy and path you take to get up the mountain—the process of accumulation—is going to be different than the strategy and path you take to get down the mountain—the process of retirement distribution.

Let's look at the differences in accumulation planning and distribution planning in more detail.

The Accumulation Phase

The accumulation phase begins when you enter the workforce and continues until retirement. During this phase, a lot is likely happening—getting married, having children, buying homes, perhaps starting a business, etc. Financially, you are (or should be) saving and investing for your short-term, mid-term, and long-term goals. This may include saving for your children's college education or paying off debt, such as existing student loans or a mortgage. It could also be to save for vacations, building an emergency fund, or perhaps acquiring a vacation home—but most importantly, saving and investing to establish a secure retirement.

During the accumulation phase, your financial objective should consist of both saving and investing. Remember, saving is for your safe money and generally involves little to no principal risk, whereas, investing involves risk to your principal. You will likely be saving and investing for many years, even decades. In addition, there are usually ways to help lower the amount of taxes you pay on your income (e.g., pre-tax 401(k) contributions or deducting the interest on a mortgage). You may think that market volatility is not much of a concern because you may be able to buy low, when the market is down, plus you have a long-term time horizon. That being said, remember you still want to consider including less volatile and low-correlated investment strategies into your plan. As you learned in Chapter 2, the math justifies this. In fact, as you explore all phases of your retirement planning, you should put more trust in the math versus opinion every time.

In addition to saving and investing, you will very likely have the need to acquire different types of insurance policies to protect you and your family from catastrophic risks. This may include disability insurance, health insurance, and life insurance. You should not gamble with these financial risks by having inadequate, or even no, disability, health, or life insurance. It's very important to obtain the appropriate types of insurance protection with sufficient coverage.

Also, during the accumulation phase, you are trying to learn how to properly manage your finances. Wall Street, the big brand-name and discount brokerage firms, media pundits, the internet, and financial advisors all provide you with an often overwhelming amount of financial and investment advice. The overall emphasis is mostly on how and where to grow your money to get to retirement. For example, you'll get advice to "max out" your 401(k) contributions or contribute to traditional or Roth IRAs. You are also strongly encouraged to invest in stocks, mutual funds, exchange-traded funds (ETFs), etc. and constantly advised on how to earn the highest rates of return. You may also hear about how to receive tax-free withdrawals or cash flow. This could be done by contributing to a Roth IRA or cash value life insurance, for example.

During the accumulation phase, if you make mistakes (and we all do), hopefully you learn from them. You have the opportunity and time to try to educate yourself or seek the proper professional advice (ideally, from an independent financial advisor), so you can fix those mistakes and make more appropriate decisions moving forward. At worst, you can possibly work a little longer or save a little more in order to make up for them. Just keep in mind that you will likely incur setbacks. That's life! You may have a great plan in place for your long-term savings and investment goals, then something happens that derails that plan. This could be the need to help out a relative or friend financially. Perhaps you lose your job or have a medical issue that incur unexpected out-of-pocket expenses. Your car could have mechanical issues that need repair work or needs to be traded in for a new one. You understand my point—these types of unforeseen things can and do happen. Therefore, you should certainly anticipate and plan for them. But you also don't have to let them completely derail your retirement planning either.

Summary of what people generally do during the accumulation phase:
- Save and invest for retirement such as through a 401(k) and/or IRA.
- Take more investment risk and seek the highest rate of return.
- Invest in the stock market with stocks, mutual funds, or ETFs.
- Incur debt such as a mortgage on a home, financing on a car (or two),

college loans, unpaid credit card balances, etc.
- Seek tax breaks to reduce taxable income.
- Seek out employee benefits an employer may offer such as health insurance, company match to a 401(k), health savings account (HSA), etc.
- Buy life insurance and/or disability insurance for income replacement.
- If there are children, save for college.

During the accumulation phase, don't dismiss or overlook cash flow strategies as part of your growth objective. Cash flow, such as dividends and interest, for example, can be an instrumental part of your total return. It's fine to have pure growth investments, but you shouldn't rely solely on growth or appreciation. Work with an independent financial advisor on determining the appropriate balance of cash flow and growth strategies to help optimize your accumulation phase.

In addition to including cash flow strategies, based on what you have learned so far, also look to include low volatile and low market-correlated savings and investments. Of course, tailor it to your own situation and risk tolerance.

The Distribution Phase

This is the phase where you begin taking retirement income and withdrawals—your cash flow. This may be required to last for decades. In fact, there is a very realistic chance you could be taking income and withdrawals for 30 or more years, so, you need to plan accordingly for this possibility. Also, during the distribution phase, you probably will have fewer tax benefits. For example, you may likely have little to no interest to deduct assuming your mortgage may be paid off or mostly paid off. Then again, you can plan ahead to maintain a mortgage or perhaps a second home with a mortgage if you want to continue receiving the mortgage interest tax deduction (if eligible). It all comes down to deciding, with your financial advisor's guidance, what you can afford with your available cash flow during the distribution phase.

In addition, during the distribution phase, a lot will likely change with regard to where your money is allocated and your cash flow is going as compared to the accumulation phase. For example, since you're no longer working, there is no longer a need for disability insurance. Conversely, the need for long-term care insurance should be considered. And, everyone has the need for health insurance. So, even though you become eligible for Medicare at age 65, you will still incur some out-of-pocket health insurance expenses that need to be accounted for in your plan (e.g., co-pays, deductibles, and supplemental insurance premiums). Plus, if you retire prior to age 65, and you do not have a spousal health insurance plan that you can join, you will have to find and pay for an individual health insurance policy. Your premium payment will most likely be much higher than the plan that was provided by your employer.

Also, you may no longer need life insurance to replace your income in order to provide for your dependents. However, life insurance may now be useful elsewhere. For example, to provide for liquidity needs at your death. It can also help pay off any debt or tax liabilities owed by your estate or your beneficiaries, whether it's income taxes on your retirement accounts or, if applicable, estate taxes. In addition, life insurance may be used to leave a financial legacy to your children, grandchildren, or the religious or charitable organization of your choice. Therefore, when you think about life insurance, you should think long term—not just *until* retirement, but *through* your retirement as well.

The distribution phase is also where you absolutely want to emphasize cash flow over growth. It's okay to keep a portion of your retirement assets invested for growth. Just don't forget the main objective of this phase is to maximize your retirement income and to make sure it lasts your whole life. This is best accomplished by utilizing the cash flow options and strategies that will be discussed in Chapters 5, 6, and 7. As always, it's important to seek out an independent financial advisor to personally guide you through this phase based on your individual circumstances and goals.

It's also important to point out that the investments typically used during the accumulation phase such as mutual funds, target date funds, and even company stock held in your retirement accounts such as a 401(k), are not designed to provide cash flow—certainly not reliable or guaranteed cash flow that's not contingent on how the stock and bond markets perform. These investments can potentially work during the accumulation phase, but they are far too unpredictable and unreliable during the distribution phase, especially if you want to reduce risk, maximize cash flow, and not worry about running out of retirement income. Plus, investing should not be your focus or concern during the distribution phase. Your focus should be on making sure you have sufficient cash flow—that will last throughout your retirement. Having the right cash flow strategy will determine not only whether you have enough income to make it through retirement but also how comfortable your retirement could potentially be.

Some other things to consider: Do you roll over your 401(k) to an IRA? Do you convert your 401(k) or traditional IRA to a Roth IRA? When should you start Social Security? If you have a pension, should you take a lump sum payment, if that's an option, or as a monthly annuity payment and if so, when should you start the monthly annuity payment?

You must also address your current risk tolerance as it relates to market volatility, sequence of returns risk, and longevity risk (longevity risk will be discussed in Chapter 7). Furthermore, you need to also consider potential liquidity needs, applicable insurance policies and appropriate insurance coverages, and of course, how you generate cash flow for your needs and wants. I will address this further in Chapter 7 (Creating Your Ideal Retirement Plan: It's All About Cash Flow).

Note: Most financial advisors are only trained in and have experience with accumulation planning. If you're having a discussion with a financial advisor regarding your distribution planning strategy and the emphasis is on the "rate of return" that he or she can supposedly get for you and not on cash flow that provides reliable and guaranteed income, then you have the wrong advisor. That advisor is not properly trained and certainly not experienced in the area of distribution planning, nor is he or she acting as a true fiduciary.

Summary of what retirees generally do (or should do) during the distribution phase:

- Take less risk.
- Seek investments and financial products to provide cash flow for retirement income.
- Try to avoid depleting their retirement accounts.
- Seek ways to increase retirement income to keep pace with inflation.
- Consider long-term care insurance.
- Reduce or eliminate debt (e.g., pay off the mortgage).
- Downsize their home or move to a less costly area.
- Look to relocate to a warmer climate and/or buy a winter home.
- Plan to leave a financial legacy.

Remember, you will be retired and no longer have that paycheck from your employer or business. You certainly don't want to worry about running out of money or retirement income. Like the mountain climber who can't afford to make mistakes on his or her journey coming down from the summit, you can't afford any mistakes during the retirement distribution phase. You probably have only one shot at getting this right. And keep in mind, the government is not going to bail you out as they did some of the Wall Street firms and Fortune 500 companies during the Great Recession!

It's worth repeating: The financial strategies you use to get to retirement during the accumulation phase are very different from those you should be using during retirement in the distribution phase. Therefore, be sure to view and manage the accumulation and distribution phases independently of the other. Educate yourself on these differences along with which strategies will work best for you in each phase (i.e., pursue knowledge). Finally, just as the mountain climber seeks professional guidance to get to the summit and then descend from it, you too should seek professional, independent financial guidance.

Chapter 5

Think Cash Flow, Not Rate of Return

It's often said, "Cash is king." However, I say, "*Cash flow* is king." That's because cash itself isn't continuously working for you. It sits idle and earns very little, especially after inflation is factored in. Also, and more important, once you spend cash, it's gone. But cash flow keeps *flowing* in. Cash flow allows you to make the mortgage payment and car payment every month; pay your utilities and buy groceries; save for a new car, save for college and retirement; or reach whatever other goals you may have. Cash flow allows you to do all of that and more. Plus, it's certainly much more reliable than investing in the stock market to seek a rate of return.

Unfortunately, most people underestimate how vital cash flow is. They just overlook its importance and relevance, again, this is because of how they have been taught to think. However, the wealthy, business owners, and senior management of Fortune 500 companies understand how vital and relevant cash flow is. Banks do as well. In fact, banks have the concept of cash flow mastered. Think about it. Banks take in deposits and then lend out those deposits to receive cash flow from your mortgage or car payment, for example. Banks also offer credit cards, charge interest, and profit a great deal from those who end up making monthly payments, versus paying off the balance each month. In addition, car dealerships are always promoting some sort of finance or lease payment offer. One of the first things the salesperson asks you is, "How much of a monthly payment can you afford?" They never mention the cash price of the car; you usually have to ask. They not only expect you to finance or lease the vehicle, they prefer that you do. That's because financing has become more profitable for the auto industry than the sale of the cars themselves. And how about the retail stores that offer financing incentives on appliances? Even many of the cell phone carriers are now allowing you to finance the cost of the phone by adding it into your monthly service contract. This financing provides consistent cash flow to all of these businesses. They are certainly thinking in terms of cash flow.

How about Wall Street? They administer and invest the money going into 401(k) and 403(b) plans as well as IRAs, mutual funds, brokerage accounts, etc.

And every pay period, money is automatically contributed into these plans. That's consistent and reliable cash flow on which they make money through the myriad management and transaction fees they charge. Clearly, Wall Street has a cash flow strategy and not a rate of return strategy. It's now time for you to think the same way—in terms of cash flow, not rate of return.

Cash Flow versus Rate of Return: You Can't Spend Rate of Return

It's very important to understand why I say you can't spend rate of return. Let me explain by using an example of a mutual fund. If you invest in a mutual fund that doesn't pay a dividend and the mutual fund increases in value by 7 percent as a result of an increase in the share value of the mutual fund that growth is considered your rate of return.

Now let's say the mutual fund pays a dividend of 7 percent. That is cash flow. You can have the dividend paid out to you every month or quarter, depending on the mutual fund's dividend distribution frequency, to spend such as for retirement or you can reinvest it to help with the growth of your mutual fund. It also doesn't require you to sell any shares of the mutual fund. In addition, you don't have to *hope* that the mutual fund grows by 7 percent in value or worse, pray that it doesn't lose value. If the latter happens, to withdraw 7 percent in order to generate cash flow would require you to sell shares *after* the value of the mutual fund has dropped. This is an example of the consequences that result from the impact of sequence of returns risk that we explored in Chapter 2.

Let's look at some examples of all of this in action. In the first examples (rate of return), we will look at several scenarios that assume your mutual fund's rate of return is solely from market appreciation or growth. In the second examples (cash flow), we will assume your mutual fund's rate of return is solely due to a dividend distribution.[1]

In this rate of return example, if you invested $100,000 and the fund grew in value a year later by 7 percent, your mutual fund would now be worth $107,000 (excluding any applicable fees or taxes). However, if you needed a withdrawal or income in the amount of $7,000 from this investment, the only way to withdraw that $7,000 would be to sell shares equaling that amount. Here's the breakdown:

- Mutual fund: $100,000 initial investment with no dividend and a $100/share price buys 1,000 shares.
- Growth of the mutual fund's share price at 7 percent equals $107/share.
- 1,000 shares at $107/share is now valued at $107,000.

Initial investment	Price per share	Total shares owned
$100,000	$100	1,000

One year later:

Price per share	Total shares owned	Current value
$107	1,000	$107,000

Now, in order to withdraw $7,000 (7 percent growth) from the mutual fund, you must sell $7,000 worth of shares, which is approximately 65.42 shares. You are now left with 934.58 shares.

Result after selling shares to withdraw the $7,000:

Price per share	Shares sold	Amount withdrawn	Total shares owned	Current value
$107	65.42	$7,000	934.58	$100,000

In Year 2, if the mutual fund grows by another 7 percent, the value is again back to $107,000:

Price per share	Total shares owned	Current value
$114.49	934.58	$107,000

You can now sell another $7,000 worth of shares. Again, that will bring your investment value back down to $100,000. This would be great if you could count on that 7 percent growth rate *each and every year*. However, that's just not realistic.

Now, let's see what would happen if the mutual fund instead *lost* 7 percent in the first year. The share price would be $93 per share, and the value would now be only $93,000.

Initial investment	Price per share	Total shares owned
$100,000	$100	1,000

One year later:

Price per share	Total shares owned	Current value
$93	1,000	$93,000

You have no gain or positive rate of return to withdraw from, do you? If you take a withdrawal of $7,000, you will have to sell 75.27 shares (75.27 shares sold at $93/share equals $7,000). You are now left with 924.73 shares in your mutual fund account. As a result, the mutual fund value is now down to approximately $86,000:

Price per share	Shares sold	Amount withdrawn	Total shares owned	Current value
$93	75.27	$7,000	924.73	$86,000

Now, if (and that's a big *if*) the mutual fund increases by 7 percent the following year, you will have a share value of $99.51 per share, and the investment value would still be only $92,020.

End of Year 2:

Price per share	Total shares owned	Current value
$99.51	924.73	$92,020

You are nowhere near back to your original $100,000 or even the $107,000 value that was needed for your $7,000 income withdrawal. As you learned in Chapter 2, such a systematic withdrawal strategy can be very detrimental when factoring in market losses into the mix. You don't see these losses reflected or being accounted for in most retirement plan projections. You just see a constant, positive rate of return.

Now, let's take a look at the following cash flow examples.

You have a mutual fund that pays a 7 percent annualized distribution rate but, there is no growth of the share value in Year 1. (By the way, the investment doesn't have to be a mutual fund. There are many types of investments that provide cash flow that you should consider. You will be introduced to them in the next section of this chapter.) Then in Year 2, it paid another 7 percent annualized distribution rate, however, this time the investment lost 7 percent. (Please note, for simplicity, I am assuming the dividend is paid out once per year. In reality, dividends are typically paid out more frequently, such as monthly or quarterly.)

Initial investment	Price per share	Total shares owned	Distribution rate
$100,000	$100	1,000	7%

One year later:

Price per share	Total shares owned	Distribution rate	Current value
$100	1,000	$7,000	$100,000

Year 2 after 7% drop in share value:

Price per share	Total shares owned	Distribution rate	Current value
$93	1,000	$7,000	$93,000

Please note, no shares had to be sold to receive your cash flow of $7,000 in either year. The share price or investment value may fluctuate up and down, but the $7,000 annualized distribution is generally deemed more reliable. Certainly, far more reliable than depending on the growth of the share value. And, that's the point of what I mean when I say you can't spend rate of return. Rates of return are not reliable and can even be negative.

Also, if the distributions (i.e., cash flow) are not needed, you can reinvest them. Doing so can potentially increase the overall growth of the investment. That's because cash flow from an investment is a part of the rate of return. Then, once the distributions are needed (typically at retirement), you can simply elect to have them paid out to you. Remember, whether you are taking the dividends or distributions as income or reinvesting them, it's still cash flow that's *working for you*.

Sources that Generate Cash Flow

During your working years, you earn income and receive regular paychecks from your employer. If you own a business, earned income comes from distributions or profits from your business. It's generally consistent and reliable, meaning you work and your paycheck gets deposited into your checking or savings account each pay period. That's cash flow. We should all understand this. Without this consistent and reliable cash flow every pay period, we couldn't pay our rent or mortgage, pay our car loan, buy groceries, pay the utility bills, or even save and invest, such as for a future purchase, college tuition, or retirement.

Once retired, you need to replace the cash flow that was provided by that regular paycheck. You can use what has been accumulated in your retirement accounts to do this, or perhaps a pension is available to provide that cash flow. Of course, there are likely Social Security retirement benefits available as well. Regardless, during retirement, you will continue to need cash flow.

As I have already stated, cash flow isn't just about retirement income. You should be thinking cash flow throughout your entire life. As discussed in Chapter 4, utilizing cash flow even during the accumulation phase is a very prudent strategy. Remember, cash flow can be compounded or reinvested to help with the accumulation of wealth. As you learned in Chapter 3, the wealthy certainly understand this.

Now, let's take a look at the various sources that can generate cash flow.

Dividend-paying stocks, mutual funds, exchange-traded funds, and unit investment trusts. These investments provide cash flow in the form of dividends. Retirees have historically used dividends for retirement income. Unfortunately, over the years, many companies have cut or even stopped paying dividends to shareholders. That's because as the stock market flourished in the 1980s and 1990s, investing for growth in the stock market became very popular. Due to this newfound mentality to seek growth, Wall Street influenced many publicly traded companies to use their positive cash flow to reinvest back into the company in order to help further increase share value, rather than pay it out as a dividend. This strategy was also much more preferred by the companies' top executives because much of their compensation was in the form of company stock. Plus, increasing the share value of company stock is good for their job security. Investors were also taught to focus on growth and rates of return and less on dividends (i.e., cash flow). But what most people don't realize is that dividends have been a big component of an investment's rate of return over the years. In fact, according to Standard & Poor's,[2] the dividend component of the S&P 500® Index was responsible for 44 percent of the rate of return over the past 80 years of the index. Look at the two graphs on the next page to see how dividends positively impact the rate of return.

THE POWER OF DIVIDENDS AND COMPOUNDING
Growth of $10,000 (12/1960-12/2017)

Data Source: Morningstar, 1/18.

$2,571,920 represents the value of the S&P 500® with dividends reinvested.

$460,095 represents the value of the S&P 500® without dividends reinvested.

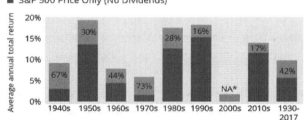

Data Source: Morningstar 1/18. *Total Return for the S&P 500 Index was negative
for the 2000s. Dividends provided a 1.8% annualized return over the decade.

Here again is Kevin O'Leary, investor on TV's *Shark Tank*, on the subject
of dividends:

> "I'm a dividend guy. I only buy stocks that pay dividends. I'll never buy a stock
> that doesn't return capital, because the data tells you not to."

As previously discussed, the use of dividends also means you don't have
to rely solely on the growth from your investment for your rate of return. For
example (and as described in the previous section), in order to get a 9 percent
rate of return in a pure growth stock or mutual fund that pays no dividend, the
stock or mutual fund will have to derive its 9 percent rate of return *completely* from
appreciation of the stock price or the mutual fund's net asset value. However, if a

stock or mutual fund paid an annualized dividend of 4 percent, for example, then the stock or mutual fund would only need to appreciate in value by 5 percent to obtain the same rate of return. If the nondividend-paying stock or mutual fund were to have no growth at all, then your rate of return is zero. However, if the dividend-paying stock or mutual fund were to have no growth, you would still have a 4 percent rate of return as a result of the 4 percent dividend. Which would you prefer, especially if you are retired and needing income?

The impact of dividends should not be overlooked. Yes, they certainly aren't guaranteed, but they can be a major contributor toward the overall growth of your investment portfolio and total rate of return in addition to being a source of cash flow.

Bonds, bond mutual funds, certificates of deposit (CDs), money markets, fixed annuities, and fixed-index annuities. Interest from these types of savings and investments can provide cash flow. However, the rate of interest earned can change over time as interest rates move up or down. For example, money market and other fixed account interest rates were much higher before the real estate market bust and stock market meltdown in 2008. The Federal Reserve then lowered interest rates to try to stabilize the economy. Those previously higher interest rates that people were accustomed to earning dropped substantially. The real disaster was for the many retirees who were relying on those interest rate levels for their retirement income. Even though interest earnings can be a source of cash flow, the interest rates that determine interest earnings do not make it a reliable source.

Systematic withdrawals from investment accounts. This strategy requires you to sell shares of stocks or mutual funds in your account, such as a 401(k) or IRA, each month to make available the cash flow to be able to withdraw. You have to be very cautious. As you have previously read, this strategy can subject you to sequence of returns risk and market volatility risk, which can lead to the possibility of depleting your account. Remember, no account value means no income or cash flow.

Real estate investments. Whether you own the actual properties and rent the unit(s), invest in real estate income mutual funds, or invest in direct-participation real estate offerings such as nontraded real estate investment trusts (nontraded REITs), this can provide cash flow. Of course, this cash flow can also be used for retirement income. In addition, the cash flow can potentially increase over time to provide a hedge against inflation.

Private loans and private equity. These investments are quite common among the wealthy. Even though these investments are generally illiquid and have varying degrees of risk associated with them, private loans in particular usually provide a higher cash flow distribution rate than cash flow from other sources such as dividends from stocks or mutual funds, or interest from bonds or CDs, in addition to their potential for growth. Private loans can also be very attractive in an environment of rising interest rates. These investments often require a minimum income or specific net worth by the investor to be able to invest in them. Also, unlike private loans, not all private equity provides cash flow.

High cash value life insurance (also called permanent life insurance). The objective of high cash value life insurance is to build up as much cash value in the policy as soon as possible to be available and accessible to you. There are various types of high cash value life insurance. One type in particular is dividend-paying whole life insurance. This type of cash value life insurance policy can provide cash flow in the form of annual dividends distributed by the insurance company. Cash flow can also be generated from withdrawals or policy loans from the cash value of the policy. (Universal life and index universal life policies don't pay dividends, but they can be structured to provide cash flow through withdrawals or policy loans as well.) The dividends are not guaranteed, however, a number of very financially strong insurance companies have paid dividends every single year for over a century. They have even paid dividends during the Great Depression of the 1930s. High cash value life insurance can be an ideal way to provide supplemental tax-free[3] retirement income. As you read in Chapter 3, this is quite common in the business and executive benefits world and among the wealthy. Also, as I previously mentioned, I use high cash value life insurance in my own personal financial plan. Understanding how it works, as well as the pros and cons, of this type of cash flow strategy is important. It is highly recommended you seek advice and assistance from an independent financial advisor who is knowledgeable on how to use the various benefits available through a high cash value life insurance policy.

Guaranteed Sources of Cash Flow

Social Security. People often rely on the cash flow from Social Security for part of their retirement income. For some, Social Security can make up most, if not all, of their retirement income. Social Security can't be taken in a lump sum. It is paid monthly and you receive it for as long as you live. Once you pass away, payments stop. If you are married, your surviving spouse can receive your payments if yours are higher, but not both payments. Potential increases in Social Security payments are linked to the consumer price index (CPI). This means that if the CPI increases, then your Social Security payment can increase as well.

Pensions. Most pensions are designed to provide a monthly payout for life (i.e., annuity payment) that is usually determined by a formula based on the length of service with your employer and your annual earnings or salary (e.g., highest five years of salary). This type of pension is also called a defined benefit plan.

There are different types of pension plans, but for the most part they are set up to pay the retired employee a lifetime income (i.e., annuity) during retirement. If you are married and elect the spousal option, your surviving spouse will continue to receive the lifetime annuity after your death. The actual amount your surviving spouse receives is based on certain factors determined at the time you elected to start your pension benefit. For those fortunate enough to have a pension plan, and who worked for that employer long enough, this could likely provide you with a substantial source of your retirement cash flow.

Unfortunately, there generally isn't an option in the private sector for the monthly pension payments to increase in order to keep pace with inflation. (Some state and federal pensions do provide annual or cost of living increases.) Also, if your employer provides retiree medical insurance and deducts that cost from your pension payments, the risk is that those pension payments could actually be reduced in order to cover the likely possibility of increasing retiree medical premiums. Furthermore, when you pass away, payments, other than possibly to your surviving spouse, generally stop. Nothing would go to your other beneficiaries such as children, grandchildren, other family members, charities, etc. You also don't have the flexibility to change the monthly payment amount once you start receiving your pension benefit. Some plans allow you to take a one-time, lump sum payment at the time you make your pension benefit election. The benefit to this option is that it gives you far more control and flexibility over the funds. You can then save or invest those funds as you see fit. You can even create your own personalized private pension plan, which you'll learn more about in the next chapter.

Annuities. There are many types of annuities. Some can provide guaranteed lifetime income[4] immediately such as single premium immediate annuities (SPIAs), while others are set up to defer income to the future such as deferred income annuities (DIAs) or as they are also called, longevity annuities. Variable, fixed, and fixed-index annuities are types of tax-deferred annuities that can also provide guaranteed lifetime income if converted into an immediate annuity (i.e., annuitized). In addition, many variable and fixed-index annuities offer a guaranteed lifetime income benefit rider, which is an optional feature added to the annuity for the purpose of providing guaranteed lifetime income either immediately or at a future date. There is usually an additional fee when a guaranteed lifetime income benefit rider is added to the annuity.

The income or cash flow from annuities can be fixed or variable (variable income options usually come with a floor or minimum income payout). It can also be increasing. An annuity that provides increasing income can be a preset, increasing amount, such as 2 percent, 3 percent, or even 5 percent each year, or it could be based on the interest the annuity earned in a given year. Sometimes the increase in income is based on whether the annuity's investment value increased during the year. It's important to note that not all annuities need to be used as a source for income or cash flow. Some can simply be used for your accumulation goals. With all the different types of annuities available, there is most likely an annuity that can fit within your financial plan to help meet your financial objectives.

Annuities also help protect your retirement income against sequence of returns risk and market volatility risk. They can also help maximize your retirement income withdrawals without the risk of losing that income due to market loss, for example. That's why comparing them to other investments, such as mutual funds, is a huge mistake. Remember, mutual funds are simply investments that can provide for potential growth, and perhaps pay a dividend, but can also potentially lose value or stop generating that cash flow. Annuities and stock market investments are an "apples and oranges" comparison, therefore, you should not compare them. In a nutshell, you should view annuities simply as the ability to insure against outliving your retirement income. They are essentially a risk transfer tool.

Just as you diversify among stocks, bonds, mutual funds, asset classes, etc. you should diversify among financial products (e.g., annuities). That's what the wealthy do. It's simply a prudent strategy. By learning the pros and cons from reliable and truly independent sources, you can then confidently make the most appropriate decisions for you and your family.

In reviewing all of this, which I know can be a lot to absorb, the very important question you need to ask yourself is, would you rather self-manage (i.e., self-insure) the potential risk of outliving your retirement income or would you rather outsource that risk by purchasing an annuity? I feel it's very important that you take the time to understand what that risk actually is to you and retirement plan—and not just for you, but for your spouse or other dependents during retirement. Keep in mind, the right choice doesn't have to be either/or. It could very well be a combination of taking on some of the risk and outsourcing the rest. I usually find that a combination of the two is the more appropriate and comfortable strategy for most people. Remember, there is no right or wrong answer here. The right choice is actually quite simple—it's what is most appropriate based on the risk you are willing or not willing to take based on *your* situation.

As you get closer to retirement, it may be time to be honest with yourself and have that candid conversation with an independent financial advisor in order to learn about annuities. I will discuss how annuities with a guaranteed lifetime income benefit rider work in more detail in Chapter 6. If you truly appreciate and value the idea of guaranteed lifetime income, maximizing that guaranteed lifetime income, having some flexibility of the income and the asset generating the guaranteed lifetime income, and other potential benefits and features, then the next chapter is a must-read. Don't shortchange yourself. This is *your* retirement. Not Wall Street's or the big brand-name or discount brokerage firms and not the media pundits'. Just like the descent from the summit discussed in Chapter 4, you will likely have just one shot at doing this right. There are no "do overs" when it comes to the retirement distribution phase.

———————

[1] The distribution rate is not guaranteed. Distributions can potentially increase, decrease, or be eliminated. Once a dividend has been declared or announced, the share price will often increase roughly the same amount as the dividend. This is because investors who own the stock want to be paid the dividend. If they sell before the dividend is paid, they will miss out. Therefore, the only way they will sell before the dividend is actually paid is if the share price is higher than it was before the dividend was declared. Investors purchasing shares are okay paying a higher price at this point because they will be paid the dividend, which covers the premium they paid. However, once the dividend is paid, the opposite occurs, and the stock price will often fall. The price typically falls by the same amount as the dividend. Since the seller was paid the dividend, they don't need to sell for a higher amount. Plus, an investor purchasing the stock would no longer be entitled to the dividend, so they aren't willing to pay a premium. Therefore, the price is typically reduced by the amount of the dividend.

[2] https://www.valuewalk.com/2017/05/dividends-responsible-44-sp-500-returns-last-80-years/

[3] Withdrawals up to the basis and policy loans are considered tax-free under current tax law.

[4] Based on the claims-paying ability of the insurer.

Chapter 6

Never Outlive Your Retirement Income:
Create Your Own Personalized Private Pension Plan

The way to create your own personalized private pension plan is with an annuity. An annuity is simply a retirement product designed to pay out a steady stream of income, or as you now know to call it—cash flow. Annuities are certainly not new. They have actually been around for centuries (not years or decades, but *centuries*). Most important, they are very similar to a pension plan in that they provide guaranteed lifetime income. In fact, the United States Treasury Department has noted that annuities are the only product on the market that consumers can purchase on their own that offer guaranteed income or cash flow. Not bad!

The "Love" for Guaranteed Income
People love their Social Security and pension checks. For many, this may be their major source or only source of retirement income. Why do people love their Social Security and pensions so much? Because they provide reliable and guaranteed cash flow every month. That cash flow represents security and peace of mind to them. What's not to like about that? Furthermore, when one's retirement cash flow comes from Social Security and/or a pension, there's no worry about what's going on in the stock market, with interest rates, or the state of the economy because the retiree still gets his/her Social Security or pension deposit every month. But… hmm… isn't that exactly what an annuity does too? Actually yes, it is *exactly* what an annuity does!

People love these features and benefits when it's called Social Security or a pension, yet some seem to reject them when it's called an annuity. In fact, in an April 2018 study by the Insured Retirement Institute (IRI), "Baby Boomer Expectations for Retirement," found that 70 percent of baby boomers say it is somewhat or very important to have a source of guaranteed lifetime income other than Social Security. Yet, only 14 percent say they would purchase an annuity providing guaranteed lifetime income and only 3 percent have done it. Think about that. The solution is rejected simply because of what it's called. This makes no sense at all. Why is that? It is because of how we have been taught to think about annuities from Wall Street, the big brand-name and discount brokerage firms, and the media pundits which, unfortunately, has been based on false or misleading information. Again, it always goes back to how we have been taught to think. As I have been saying, it's time to think differently. That's why it's so important to do the independent research based on the facts and the math so you obtain the knowledge to think differently.

Addressing the Unsubstantiated and False Claims About Annuities

Why does Wall Street, the big brand-name and discount brokerage firms, and most of the media often portray annuities in a negative context? Well, it's actually not that surprising; annuities represent competition to Wall Street and the big brand-name and discount brokerage firms even though the investments they offer have completely different features and objectives than annuities, and therefore, they shouldn't even be competing in the first place. But because there are literally hundreds of billions of dollars[1] going into various types of annuity products each year, Wall Street and the big brand-name and discount brokerage firms wants those dollars, and they have done practically everything they can to get them, including the use of negative marketing tactics against annuities.

The truth is these negative marketing tactics against annuities are just a means to mask or deflect their own shortcomings. By that I mean their inability to maximize retirement income and still provide guarantees, as annuities do. This is simply something they are not able to do.

Here is what Michael Finke, professor and coordinator of the doctoral program in personal financial planning at Texas Tech University says, "A competitively priced variable annuity product is hard to beat compared to an unprotected investment portfolio. Income from a variable annuity can provide a paycheck in retirement that lasts forever."[2] Wall Street and the big brand-name and discount brokerage firms can't guarantee this the same way that insurance companies that offer annuities do.

Wall Street and the big brand-name and discount brokerage firms also want to try and convince you that they can provide you with not only higher returns but with lower fees. I find this ironic since Wall Street, in particular, is notorious for the high fees that they charge. They also claim to possess the ability, through their self-proclaimed "investment expertise," to help you generate lifetime income, but all they are doing is using systematic withdrawals or paying out dividends and/or interest with their *in-house* stock and/or bond portfolios. However, you've already seen the risk of using those strategies. The truth is, they simply can't help you generate lifetime income, not without risk to you. Remember, Wall Street and the big brand-name and discount brokerage firms are not in the business to insure against risk the way insurance companies that offer annuities do.

Providing guarantees also requires reserves mandated by the industry's regulators when insuring risk. Insurance companies are required to maintain a certain level of assets in reserves in order to help hedge some of the risk they manage. Wall Street and the big brand-name and discount brokerage firms don't want to tie up assets in reserves. They do not profit from it. They are, however, required by law to maintain reserves on the banking side of their business. Interestingly, a good portion of those reserves they are required to hold are in high cash value life insurance, the same cash value life insurance that Wall Street and the big brand-name and discount brokerage firms say to avoid. Yet, they own it and so do their wealthy clients.

It's also important to note that Wall Street and the big brand-name and discount brokerage firms are not in the business of distribution planning for retirees. That's because the distribution of their customer's assets for retirement income decreases the profits to these firms because now there is less of it invested. They are simply in the business of accumulating assets and new accounts in order to invest them in the stock market. Since they are not in the business of distribution planning, they shouldn't be considered a reliable or helpful source to provide you with the proper guidance and advice you need and should expect, especially in regard to how annuities can fit into your distribution plan.

The media is also a huge contributor to the negativity on annuities. Most of the media has written articles about annuities that are based on false, incorrect, and even misleading information. I know because I read these articles all the time. As I explained in the misconception from Chapter 1 (Media pundits provide objective and real-world financial and investment advice that's right for each person's unique situation), they can say and write virtually anything without any accountability or even having to substantiate their claims. The media are certainly not experts on annuities and their views are often based on apples-to-oranges comparisons which does not benefit the consumer at all.

You may have heard of Ken Fisher or seen his ads in magazines, the newspapers, or on television. He is the founder and chairman of Fisher Investments and also a long-time media pundit.

Ken Fisher says he "hates" annuities. He has been running a huge marketing campaign with a picture of him, and in quotes it reads, "I hate annuities and you should too." The reason he says he hates annuities is because he'd prefer you let him, through his big brand-name investment firm, manage your retirement money by investing it in the stock market. According to Fisher, he can provide you with higher rates of return. Of course, that includes the risks that comes along with it. But somehow that always seems to get omitted in his advertisements.

You want to hear a little secret? Ken Fisher doesn't really hate annuities. He actually *loves* them. That's because he has used his negative campaigning against annuities to solicit existing annuity holders to surrender or cash out of their annuities (oftentimes having to pay surrender penalties in the process) and move the proceeds over to his investment firm where they are then invested in the stock market.

His ads remind me of those negative campaign ads during election years. Those ads always seem to focus on why we should not vote for a certain candidate's opponent rather than on why we should vote *for* that candidate. Whether they are true or not is often debatable. Honestly, I'd much rather hear about why we should vote for a candidate than why we shouldn't vote for the opposing candidate. In the same way, I'd much rather hear about why we should put our money in a company's financial product than why we shouldn't put our money in another company's financial product. The irony is that these negative advertisements against annuities have surely helped increase the assets that his firm manages and therefore his income too. Think about it, why would he continue to run those negative ads against annuities if doing so weren't profitable for him?

Fisher also states that his firm can help you obtain "higher" withdrawal rates when you retire because you'll be invested in the stock market. Of course, you the investor, takes on 100 percent of the risk. This sounds exactly like the advice from Wall Street, the big brand-name and discount brokerage firms, Suze Orman, and Dave Ramsey, doesn't it? Sadly, they can be quite convincing. Remember, if it sounds too good to be true, it probably isn't true.

So, the next time you see one of Fisher's "I hate annuities" advertisements, you can simply dismiss them and smile because you now know the truth; in a self-serving way, he actually *loves* annuities. In fact, he loves them so much he has even bought shares of stock in companies of several of the largest distributors of annuities ("Ken Fisher, famous annuity hater, invested in annuity companies", August 31, 2018, *Investment News*).

Wall Street, the big brand-name and discount brokerage firms, and most of the media pundits will also say these annuities charge "excessive" fees and that you can get other investments with much lower fees. STOP RIGHT THERE! A variable annuity and fixed-index annuity with a guaranteed lifetime income benefit rider are *not* investments. They are not stocks, nor bonds, nor mutual funds. A variable annuity and fixed-index annuity with a guaranteed lifetime income benefit rider are financial products that provide guaranteed lifetime income withdrawals. They are actually better classified as a pension alternative or a risk transfer tool—which is what these financial products are designed to be. Stocks, bonds, and mutual funds certainly are not. When these annuities are compared to at-risk investments like these, it is inappropriate and even misleading.

As I have repeatedly stated, there is no free lunch. The reason a variable annuity and fixed-index annuity with a guaranteed lifetime income benefit rider can provide the features, benefits, and guarantees I've mentioned is because you are going to pay an additional fee. But you need to view this additional fee in its proper context, which is like an insurance premium. This "premium" is simply the cost to insure against running out of income from the annuity, which is why I adamantly disagree with the statement that the fees are "excessive." Instead, you should be asking yourself, "What am I getting for the additional fee I am paying?" If there is a benefit or value, then it's probably well worth it. For most retirees, this is a benefit and provides value. This is also another great example illustrating that cheaper is not always better. This being said, there are some annuities that have lower external fees compared to some investment portfolios or mutual funds once *all* fees—such as operating expenses, transaction costs, and investment advisor fees are factored in.

It's also very important to note that the fees charged by the annuity are not deducted from your income withdrawal base or from your guaranteed lifetime income withdrawal amount. All fees are deducted from the account value only. This is a very important distinction.

It is true that variable and fixed-index annuities, or annuities in general, can sometimes be complicated or not easy to understand, so don't worry or feel embarrassed if you don't grasp this at first. There is often a learning curve. I completely understand this is likely all new to you. That is why, when I explain annuities to clients, I am very patient and spend sufficient time educating them on how they work as well as the pros and cons. However, you have to ask yourself how much do you really understand the stock market, mutual funds, bonds, bond mutual funds, and all the other different investments out there? Be honest with yourself. Just because you have had those types of investments for many years doesn't necessarily mean you understand how they work. I have found this often to be the case. The reality is, it's quite easy to get comfortable with what you have always been doing. After all, these investments are all you've been aware of and have been advised to invest your money in. Plus, "everyone else" is doing it too, right? (Although, I already explained why that is not an acceptable or prudent reason.) Then, as you approach retirement, you are introduced to something completely new—annuities. This is a perfect time to remind you how important it is to seek out knowledge and not just information (or misinformation) from the internet, Wall Street, the big brand-name and discount brokerage firms, or many of the media pundits. Follow the facts and the math instead.

The truth is, once you do understand and start using annuities, they are really no longer that complicated. There is also not that much to manage as you do with Wall Street's and the big brand-name and discount brokerage firms' investments. The annuity simply pays you a guaranteed lifetime monthly income that can also possibly increase, but not decrease. The only "management" needed is to decide which investment(s) or market index (indices) you want from among the choices offered (assuming that you are using a variable or fixed-index annuity). Even this doesn't have to be complicated or actively managed. With help from your independent financial advisor, you can simply select from one of the diversified portfolio models offered in the variable annuity, or in the case of a fixed-index annuity, one or more of the various market indices available based on your risk tolerance. That's it! Once you select the type of annuity that's most appropriate for you, choose the investments or market indices, and decide when to start taking income, the "hard" part is pretty much over—quite unlike stocks, bonds, mutual funds, etc. that still needs to be watched over and managed due to the risks associated with them.

Finally, if someone gives you their opinion on annuities, and they say something like, "they're bad" or "they're complicated" or "they have high fees", ask them why and where did they hear that. It's almost certain these naysayers got their misleading or false information from the internet, their accountant, a banker, a friend, a Wall Street broker, an investment representative from a big brand-name or discount brokerage firm, or a media pundit like Suze Orman or Dave Ramsey. The likelihood that they truly understand annuities is slim to none. Therefore, you are only doing yourself a huge disservice by taking their opinion seriously. You will just end up with wrong information and bad advice. Instead, you are much better off to follow the math and facts taught by the true experts such as Dr. Moshe Milevsky and Tom Hegna, for example. They have done a great deal of real-world research on the topics of longevity risk, lifetime income planning, stock market and volatility risk, sequence of returns risk, sustainable withdrawal rates for retirees, and why you should consider an annuity in the retirement distribution phase. They have the credentials and knowledge. I encourage you to reread this chapter and the misconception from Chapter 1: I can get good financial and investment advice from my cousin, father, boss, accountant, etc. to help solidify your knowledge and understanding on this. As the saying goes: Knowledge is power! Don't be afraid of annuities. Instead, be afraid of outliving your retirement income.

The Personalized Private Pension Plan

In the last chapter, I shared various sources that provide cash flow including annuities. Now, let's take a look in more detail at a specific type of annuity that provides guaranteed cash flow for life—a variable annuity with a guaranteed lifetime income benefit rider.

During my many years as a financial advisor, I have met with hundreds of people planning for their retirement. What I have learned from these many discussions is that most people share common goals regarding their retirement objectives. Here is what they primarily ask for their retirement funds to provide:

- Less risk (compared to the accumulation phase)
- Access to their funds in case of an emergency
- Growth of their retirement funds
- Rising income to keep pace with inflation
- Flexibility and control
- The ability to leave any remaining funds to their beneficiaries
- Little or no reliance on the performance of the stock market
- And last and most requested, to receive lifetime income that won't run out, regardless of how long they and their spouse live (i.e., guaranteed cash flow)

What they are really asking for is what a variable annuity with a guaranteed lifetime income benefit rider provides. Think about it. Most people like the idea of the guaranteed lifetime income (or cash flow) that a traditional pension provides. However, most traditional pensions only provide a fixed payout and many of the above objectives are not available with traditional pensions. The question is, can all of the above benefits and features that people preparing for retirement want actually be obtained? Absolutely! Now, if you ask that investment representative who works for Wall Street or one of the big brand-name or discount brokerage firms, their response will be something like this: "Sure, we can manage your money to accomplish all of those objectives, no problem at all." It's very interesting how they always seem to promise high returns, "best in class" investment and financial advice, liquidity, the claim of low fees, and the ability to manage your retirement so your investments and retirement income will last for as long as you (and your spouse) live. Sounds great, doesn't it? But doesn't it also sound too good to be true? It certainly does to me, and it should to you. But that's what their financial and investment advice is, too good to be true. Do not fall for it! Never forget, there is no free lunch.

Before we look at a variable annuity with a guaranteed lifetime income benefit rider in more detail, let's look at how a traditional pension works. This will help you better understand the variable annuity with a guaranteed lifetime income benefit rider and why you would want to consider such an annuity in the first place.

The Basics of a Traditional Pension Plan

The following is how a pension plan generally works. The employer periodically contributes to the company's pension plan with the goal of eventually paying out lifetime income to the future retirees of the company. The payout to retired employees is usually based on their years of service and highest average salary (e.g., the highest five years of salary) with the company. The investment manager of the pension then invests the contributions for two main objectives: growth of the overall pension assets and the ability to generate lifetime income (cash flow) when each employee retires.

The following is important to note: whether the pension plan's investment results do extremely well or extremely poorly, it will have no impact on the retiree's monthly pension check. The retirees in the pension plan continue to receive the same amount regardless of the pension plan's investment performance. It is also important to note that there is some risk, but also some protections, should the company go into bankruptcy. A discussion with a financial advisor and/or the company's pension plan administrator is recommended to understand this in more detail. The main point, however, is that the investment performance of the pension plan, whether good or bad, will generally have no impact with regard to the retiree's monthly pension check.

When the employee eventually retires, the pension plan will provide an annuity (yes, an annuity!) payout to the retired employee. This can be in the form of a single life annuity, joint and survivor annuity, or period certain annuity. The pension plan summary description or your financial advisor can explain how the available annuity payout options work.

Sometimes the pension manager may outsource the risk of the annuity payment to an insurance company (the same insurance companies where *you,* too, can purchase an annuity). More and more pension plans are opting for this due to numerous factors such as historically low interest rates, the impact of recent stock market crashes, and the expectation of lower returns in the stock market. In addition, companies are contributing less to their pension plans. All of this has created a great deal of pressure on the investment managers of pension plans. These investment managers realize there is only so much that they can do, especially given the current financial environment. They understand that outsourcing the risk is a very prudent financial strategy for all parties involved. (With regard to your own retirement assets, don't be afraid to outsource the risk either. If investment managers of pension plans can do it, you certainly can do it too.) What ultimately needs to be understood is that the retiree is receiving his or her lifetime income in the form of an *annuity* payment. The retiree and, if applicable, his or her spouse will receive these annuity checks for life. That sounds really good, doesn't it? After all, that's what retirement income is supposed to provide, right?

However, this is where the benefit of a lifetime annuity from a pension ends. That's because the retiree doesn't have access to the account value should they ever need it. Also, most private pension plans' retirement annuity benefits do not increase over time to keep pace with inflation. The pension payments remain the same. In addition, when the retired employee dies, and their spouse dies (assuming a joint survivor option was elected), the pension payments come to an end. Generally, there is no payout to beneficiaries. Nothing goes to their children, grandchildren, family members, etc.

There are some pension plans that allow the retired employee to take a one-time lump sum payment in lieu of the monthly annuity payments. This lump sum payment is generally based on a formula that calculates the present value for a single life annuity the retiree would have received at age 65. The retired employee can then take the lump sum payment and either (a) pay income taxes on it or (b) roll it into an IRA account in order to continue to defer the taxes. The decision on whether to take the monthly annuity or a lump sum payment (if that is an option) is a big one. Just like any investment or financial decision, it's very important to understand the pros and cons.

If you were to elect the lump sum payment option, imagine being able to:

- put the money into an account that provides guaranteed lifetime income, like a traditional pension plan does,
- potentially increase your guaranteed lifetime income if the investments in the annuity do well enough, unlike a traditional pension plan

and…

- leave any remaining value to your beneficiaries, again, unlike a traditional pension plan.

Wouldn't that be great? Interested?

Well, that is exactly what you can get, plus more, if you take the lump sum payment from the pension (or funds from any other retirement asset or account, such as your 401(k), 403(b), mutual funds, cash, etc.) and put it into a variable annuity with a guaranteed lifetime income benefit rider. This allows you to achieve your primary retirement objective, which is guaranteed income for life. In addition, you have the potential for your retirement income payout to increase if the investments selected in the variable annuity increase above the *income withdrawal base*.[3] The income withdrawal base is a value that is used in the calculation of your guaranteed lifetime income amount each year. Furthermore, if the investments selected in the variable annuity lose value, or even lose all their value, there is no risk of losing your guaranteed lifetime retirement income withdrawals.[4] Your guaranteed income essentially gets the *upside* potential but none of the *downside* risk with a variable annuity with a guaranteed lifetime income benefit rider. Remember, with a traditional pension, whether the investments in the plan gain or lose value, it doesn't change your monthly income, whereas the variable annuity with a guaranteed lifetime income benefit rider does provide the potential for growth of your income without the risk of your income ever declining.

Tell me what investment that Wall Street or the big brand-name or discount brokerage firms sell does this? You can't, because there isn't one. The truth is, these firms can only offer the *hope* of high returns, but that comes with risk to you and your retirement funds. Both pensions and annuities offer what they can't—guaranteed lifetime income, which is exactly what most retirees want. At the very least, they want this for a portion of their retirement income. Most retirees do not want to take risk just for the *hope* of potentially higher returns with their hard-earned retirement money. Also, when using a variable annuity, you can generally access the account value as long as there are still funds available to withdraw (surrender charges may apply for a period of time). This also applies to fixed-index annuities and cash refund immediate annuities. This, however, may reduce your guaranteed lifetime income withdrawals going forward, but, the point is, it still can be an available option, which is clearly better than not having this option at all.

Furthermore, if you don't live long into retirement, the account value in the variable annuity will go to your beneficiaries. On the other hand, if you are fortunate to live for many years in retirement, you'll never have to worry about running out of retirement income from the variable annuity. This applies even if the account value depletes to zero. Still, if the account value has a balance remaining in it after many years, it is available to pass on to your beneficiaries. To clarify, beneficiaries receive the account value, *not* the income withdrawal base. The income withdrawal base is simply the value that determines the amount of guaranteed lifetime income you can withdraw. I will explain exactly how the income withdrawal base works in the next section.

If you invest in any of Wall Street's or the big brand-name or discount brokerage firm's options, such as stocks, bonds, mutual funds, etc. or you put your money into CDs or money markets at the bank or credit union, and the value depletes to zero due to market losses or withdrawing in excess of your earnings, you will no longer receive a retirement check from those savings or investments. With those savings and investments, if there is no account value, then there is no income. It's that simple. However, if the account value in your variable annuity with a guaranteed lifetime income benefit rider depletes to zero, you will still continue to receive your monthly retirement check. How is that for peace of mind?

The Pension Alternative

Now let's look at an example of how a variable annuity with a guaranteed lifetime income benefit rider works.

Let's say you have the option of a lump sum payment from your pension and the amount is $500,000. (Remember, you can also do this with your 401(k), IRA, or any other retirement funds.) Your personal objectives for this money are as follows:

- Defer taking retirement income for 10 years
- Potential growth of the account value
- Prevent market losses from negatively impacting your retirement income

- Potentially increase retirement income
- Have access to the account value
- Leave any remaining account value to your beneficiaries
- Provide guaranteed lifetime income (no matter how long you live)

After thorough independent research, you determine that a variable annuity with a guaranteed lifetime income benefit rider[5] can provide all of the above objectives and is an appropriate place for this portion of your retirement funds.

The following is one way you can reach these objectives.

You rollover the $500,000 from the pension lump sum into an IRA that goes into a variable annuity with a guaranteed lifetime income benefit rider. While you defer taking your retirement income withdrawals, the insurance company where you placed the variable annuity will apply an annual credit (also called a roll-up) to your initial deposit of $500,000. This occurs on each anniversary date following the initial purchase date of the annuity. For example, if you purchased the annuity on June 5, the credit will be applied on June 5 of the following year. Keep in mind, this credit is applied to your income withdrawal base and not your account value. Also, this credit is not considered interest earnings like with a CD or money market. The credit is simply an internal accounting calculation the insurance company uses to determine the value of your income withdrawal base each year. The income withdrawal base, along with your age and whether you are taking single or joint life income withdrawals, is used to calculate the amount of your guaranteed lifetime income each year.

Now, let's assume the annual credit is 5 percent (each insurance company's crediting method will vary). One year later on the contract anniversary, your income withdrawal base will increase from $500,000 to $525,000 (5 percent of $500,000 is $25,000, which, when added to the initial $500,000, equals $525,000). Again, to be perfectly clear, this 5 percent or $25,000 credit is *not* interest earned, nor is it credited to your account value. It is *only* applied to the income withdrawal base. If you were to start taking lifetime income withdrawals after the first year, your guaranteed lifetime income would now be based on $525,000, not $500,000 nor the current account value (assuming it was less than $525,000). This credit continues to be applied each year until your *first* withdrawal or up to a maximum number of years or age (e.g., 10 years or age 80).

If you defer taking your retirement income from this annuity for 10 years, assuming the 5 percent credit and assuming it was compounded (some companies provide a compounding interest credit to the income withdrawal base, while others provide a simple interest credit), then the income withdrawal base would be $814,447 at the very minimum. ($500,000 compounded annually at 5 percent for 10 years equals $814,447[6]).

Think about it. This is actually quite a good position to be in; to know, without question, exactly what the income withdrawal base will grow to and how much guaranteed lifetime retirement income you will be able to receive at a specific point in the future. Remember, this is regardless of how the stock market did, direction of interest rates, or the state of the economy. To me, this is a very compelling proposition. And I think most people, if they are being honest with themselves, would agree.

But we're not done yet. There's more! Let's go back to the above example at the first-year anniversary. Remember, the $500,000 initial deposit with a 5 percent credit after the first year would now have an income withdrawal base of $525,000, even if the account value declined due to any loss of market value (or the account value increased but earned less than 5%). Keep in mind, this is your worst-case scenario. However, markets do go up. The question is, do you get the upside if that happens? Absolutely!

Now, let's assume the account value grows 10 percent (net of fees) after the first year. Not only is your account value $550,000 (10 percent of $500,000 is $50,000, which, when added to the initial $500,000 deposit, equals $550,000), but now, so is your income withdrawal base. You see, whichever is the *higher* value between the account value and income withdrawal base value now becomes your new income withdrawal base at your variable annuity's contract anniversary date. Your annual statement would now reflect an account value of $550,000 *and* an income withdrawal base of $550,000 as well. This is referred to as a *step-up*. That is when the income withdrawal base increases due to the account value being higher than the income withdrawal base as a result of market growth. The next question is: What happens if the account value drops in the following year as a result of a decline in the stock market? For example, the account value drops from $550,000 to $530,000. The good news is that your income withdrawal base does *not* decline. Only the account value can decline. But the further good news is, your income withdrawal base actually continues to increase (assuming no withdrawals were made). In fact, it would increase to $577,500. That's because you would receive another 5 percent credit based off the *stepped-up* income withdrawal base from the prior year, which was $550,000 ($550,000 multiplied by 5 percent added to the $550,000 equals $577,500).

Once you start taking your guaranteed lifetime income withdrawals (or any withdrawal), these annual credits generally stop. However, there still is the possibility for your income withdrawal base to increase. As a result, so would your guaranteed lifetime income; it's just not automatic. This would occur if the account value in any subsequent year grows above the income withdrawal base as of the contract anniversary. Your income withdrawal base would then reset and adjust up to equal the higher account value and thus provide even more retirement income going forward. This, too, is called a step-up.

This higher income withdrawal base is now locked in going forward even if the account value declines the following year or any year thereafter. Remember, regardless of your account value, your guaranteed lifetime income withdrawal amount does not decline. It will continue the same payout, year after year, for as long as you live. This can also extend to your spouse if you elected the joint lifetime income option. Here is an extreme, yet possible, example: If the account value ever depleted to zero, you would still receive your same guaranteed lifetime income withdrawals. The only difference is that you would no longer have money available in the account value, and therefore you could not cash out or pass anything on to your beneficiaries.

As you can see, the income withdrawal base is an extremely important component of a variable annuity with a guaranteed lifetime income benefit rider. Unfortunately, I often find that people will place more emphasis on the account value than the income withdrawal base. Doing so misses the whole point of a variable annuity with a guaranteed lifetime income benefit rider. Remember, this is about creating guaranteed cash flow. That cash flow is determined by the income withdrawal base and not by the account value which is determined by rates of return. Therefore, be sure to place more emphasis on the income withdrawal base than the account value because your main objective with this type of annuity is to create your own personalized private pension plan.

The following are two hypothetical examples of a variable annuity with a guaranteed lifetime income benefit rider. Hypothetical 1 illustrates a deferral phase (i.e., taking income later) and Hypothetical 2 illustrates an income withdrawal phase (i.e., taking income now).

Hypothetical 1 assumptions:
- Initial Deposit: $500,000
- Initial Income Withdrawal Base: $500,000
- Deferral Credit: 5%
- Deferring Lifetime Income Withdrawals

End Of Year	Gain/Loss[7]	Account Value	5% Deferral Credit Applied[8]	Income Withdrawal Base
1	-10%	$450,000	Yes	$525,000
2	+15%	$517,500	Yes	$551,250
3	+12%	$579,600	No	$579,600[9]
4	+6%	$614,376	No	$614,376[9]
5	-15%	$522,219	Yes	$645,094

Note that after year 5, the amount of guaranteed lifetime income will be based on the income withdrawal base of $645,094, not the $522,219 account value.

Hypothetical 2 assumptions:

- Initial Deposit: $500,000
- Initial Income Withdrawal Base: $500,000
- Joint Lifetime Income Withdrawal Rate (guaranteed lifetime income for both spouses): 5%
- Initial Withdrawal Amount: $25,000
- Start Lifetime Income Withdrawals

End Of Year	Gain/Loss[10]	Account Value	Income Withdrawal Base	Annual Withdrawal Following Year
1	+12%	$532,000	$532,000[11]	$26,600[12]
2	+15%	$581,210	$581,210[11]	$29,060[12]
3	-5%	$524,542	$581,210	$29,060
4	+18%	$584,668	$584,668[11]	$29,233[12]
5	-12%	$488,782	$584,668	$29,233
30	N/A	$0	$584,668	$29,233
35	N/A	$0	$584,668	$29,233

Note that the guaranteed lifetime income withdrawals continue in the amount of $29,233, which is based on the income withdrawal base of $584,668, for both spouses even *after* the account value depleted to zero.

In addition to using a variable annuity to provide guaranteed lifetime income, you should also consider a fixed-index annuity with a guaranteed lifetime income benefit rider. That's because it too can work as a pension alternative. Fixed-index annuities have similarities to variable annuities but also notable differences. The similarities are that they both allow access to your account value (surrender charges may apply for a period of time) and the ability to pass on the remaining account value to your beneficiaries. In addition, both types of annuities have the potential for your account value and income withdrawal base to increase. Of course, they are both designed to provide guaranteed lifetime income when a guaranteed lifetime income benefit rider is added to the annuity contract.

The differences are that fixed-index annuities do not invest your money directly in the stock market. Instead, you can earn interest based on the performance of a market index (or indices) you select (e.g., S&P 500® index). The market indices available in a fixed-index annuity are subject to one of the following: a cap, a spread, or a participation rate.[13] These caps, spreads, and participation rates limits or reduces the interest that can be earned each year. For example, if an index has a cap of 5 percent, the most interest that can be earned is 5 percent—no more, even if the actual index has earned more than 5 percent.

During the deferral phase, if the market index you select is positive for the year, both the account value and income withdrawal base will increase. However, unlike the variable annuity, if the market index is negative, the fixed-index annuity's account value will not decrease. With a fixed-index annuity, you basically get some of the upside, but none of the downside.

Also, during the income withdrawal phase, some fixed-index annuities can provide increasing income, even when the account value does not exceed the income withdrawal base. If the index is positive for the year, then your income will increase the following year—it's as simple as that.

Fixed-index annuities have lower external fees compared to variable annuities. Again, there is no free lunch. Remember, with the variable annuity, even though your account value can decline (but not your income withdrawal base), it is not subject to a cap, spread, or participation rate as a fixed-index annuity is. You can earn 100 percent of the investment growth (less investment expenses) in the variable annuity.

Fixed-index annuities can work great in conjunction with a variable annuity to provide guaranteed lifetime income. Therefore, you should consider both in your retirement plan. In fact, many economists and PhDs, such as Roger Ibbotson, are proponents of fixed-index annuities as a result of their independent research.

Each insurance company that offers variable and fixed-index annuities have different features, benefits, withdrawal rates, expenses, etc. Just like anything else, one type of annuity may work in one situation while another maybe more appropriate in a different situation.

Keep in mind, I am certainly not suggesting you put all your retirement assets in annuities. You simply need to determine how much of your retirement income you want to be stable, reliable, and guaranteed. Perhaps it's one-third. Maybe it's one-half, or two-thirds. Or it may be none, and that's okay too. Everyone's situation is different. This is a decision you and your financial advisor should work on together to create the strategy that's most appropriate for you. Just be sure to avoid a financial advisor who will blindly attempt to talk you out of considering an annuity. He or she should at least show you the pros and cons, without any bias, in order for you to make an appropriate decision that's in your best interest. In fact, in a recent interview with Jackson® (Jackson National Life Insurance Company), former US Secretary of Labor Seth Harris said: "Advisors who don't recommend annuities might not be acting in their clients' best interest. It may not be right for everybody... but annuities have to be part of that conversation to ensure that you're providing the requisite level of service to the customer." Just as I stated at the beginning of this book—Being a Fiduciary—this is exactly what a true fiduciary is supposed to do.

Here is what Dr. Moshe Milevsky, professor of finance at the Schulich School of Business at York University and an MA in mathematics and statistics, said on the topic of annuities:

"There is almost a consensus in the 'ivory tower' that annuities make sense for the consumer. There have been 2,000 articles about annuities written by card-carrying professors since the 1960s, and 99.9 percent of them are pro-annuities.... Moreover, the U.S. Department of the Treasury last year [2014] issued a statement encouraging 401(k) plans to offer annuities."

The U.S. Government Accountability Office (GAO) is an independent, nonpartisan agency that works for Congress. Their mission is to support Congress in meeting its constitutional responsibilities and help improve the performance and ensure the accountability of the federal government for the benefit of the American people. The GAO provides Congress with timely information that is objective, fact-based, nonpartisan, non-ideological, fair, and balanced. The GAO's June 2011 report to the U.S. Senate's Special Committee on Aging made several specific recommendations to help protect or improve an individual's retirement security. One of these recommendations specifically called for considering an *income-generating annuity* as part of an investor's overall retirement plan. Here is what the GAO had to say on the subject of annuities:

"Instead of opting for a lump sum payout from an employer-sponsored defined benefit plan, middle-income retirees should consider converting at least part of their savings into an inflation-adjusted annuity or choose a guaranteed stream of income from an annuity."

There are many independent sources like these in support of annuities. The question is, do you choose to believe the Wall Street brokers, big brand-name and discount brokerage representatives, and media pundits or those in academia with PhDs in finance, mathematics, and economics, the United States Treasury Department, and the GAO? I prefer to believe the latter three. At this point, I am guessing you do as well. It's only common sense.

The truth is, people want and need reliable and guaranteed income which is precisely what these annuities provide. In fact, the Insured Retirement Institute (IRI) and Jackson® conducted a 2017 study, *The Language of Retirement*, to gauge how Americans evaluate their financial preparedness for retirement. They found that 90 percent of people are very or somewhat interested in an investment product that offers lifetime income and 80 percent of people said they would purchase such an investment product providing guaranteed lifetime income, even if it cost more than an alternative. The study also found that seven in 10 retirees receiving income from an annuity are satisfied with their investment—higher than any other type of investment or retirement savings vehicle.

Ask yourself these three important questions:

1. What is it I want to accomplish with my retirement assets as I approach retirement?
2. How much risk am I willing to take with both my retirement assets and the income they will provide?
3. Do I want to outsource some, all, or none of the risks I will face in retirement?

Answering these three questions can help you in making the appropriate decisions for you and your family.

Finally, wouldn't it be nice to be able to take out the maximum amount of retirement income to spend it on whatever you want and not have to worry about running out of income? And, why limit yourself to only a 2–3 percent withdrawal rate—that is considered a safe withdrawal rate according to current research? Remember, even at these currently low recommended withdrawal rates, you still have a statistical chance of running out of money. Therefore, why make this sacrifice in retirement when you could just as easily withdraw 4–6 percent (or more) instead and have it *guaranteed* for life? That's exactly what a variable or fixed-index annuity with a guaranteed lifetime income benefit rider can do. Remember, if you plan your retirement in such a way that you'll never run out of money, you'll never have to worry about it.

---

[1] LIMRA.com

[2] ThinkAdvisor, "Why Ken Fisher is Wrong on Annuities: Milevsky, Finke," November 2015.

[3] The income withdrawal base is sometimes called the protected base or benefit base. Regardless of what the insurance company calls it, the income withdrawal base is what determines the amount of guaranteed lifetime income you can withdraw.

[4] Based on the claims-paying ability of the insurance company.

[5] This is an example of a variable annuity with a guaranteed lifetime income benefit rider. A fixed-index annuity with a guaranteed lifetime income benefit rider is also a viable option, however, it offers some different features compared with a variable annuity. Neither is necessarily better; in fact, combining both could be a prudent strategy.

[6] It's very important to understand that this $814,447 only represents the income withdrawal base. This is *not* the account value. The account value is a separate

value—the amount that you can cash out of the annuity (less any applicable surrender charges) or leave to your beneficiaries. The income withdrawal base is specifically the value upon which your guaranteed lifetime retirement income withdrawals are based.

[7] Net of fees.

[8] The income withdrawal base increases each year by the higher of: the 5% credit or the account value at contract anniversary each year until the first withdrawal. "Yes" means the 5% credit was applied to increase the income withdrawal base because the income withdrawal base was higher than the account value for the year. "No" means the 5% credit was not applied to the income withdrawal base because the account value was higher than the income withdrawal base for the year. Therefore, the year's account value growth was applied to increase the income withdrawal base instead.

[9] Step-up, due to account value being higher than income withdrawal base.

[10] Net of fees.

[11] Step-up, due to the account value being higher than the income withdrawal base, net of annual withdrawal, at contract anniversary.

[12] Increase to the guaranteed lifetime income annual withdrawal due to the income withdrawal base step-up.

[13] Cap: Some fixed-index annuities set a maximum rate of interest (or cap) that the contract can earn in a specified period (usually a month or year). If the chosen index increase exceeds the cap, the cap is used to calculate your interest. For example, if the annual cap in a hypothetical example was 3 percent and the value of the index rose by 4.80 percent, the cap amount of 3 percent would be credited to your contract. However, if the index change was 2 percent, your contract would be credited 2 percent since that is lower than our hypothetical cap.

Spread: The indexed interest for some annuities is determined by subtracting a percentage from any gain the index achieves in a specified period. For example, if the annuity has a 4 percent spread and the index increases 10 percent, the contract is credited 6 percent indexed interest.

Participation rate: In some annuities, a participation rate determines what percentage of the index increase will be used to calculate your indexed interest. For example, let's suppose the index rose by 10 percent. If a hypothetical fixed-index annuity had a 75 percent participation rate, the contract would receive 7.5 percent in indexed interest. (Participation rates are generally applied after caps, and before a spread.)

CHAPTER 7

Creating Your Ideal Retirement Plan: It's All About Cash Flow

The Previous Generation's Retirement

Years ago, retirement planning was much different than it is today and, in many ways, much simpler. While working, people would put any extra money into savings accounts, United States savings bonds, and even cash value life insurance policies. Furthermore, very little, if any, of their savings would be invested in the stock market, which was deemed too risky. (Hmmm... *interesting*, huh?) People typically retired around the age of 65. At that time, they would likely begin to collect Social Security retirement benefits, and if they had one, a monthly pension. On average, people lived for only about 10 years in retirement. As a result, the stock market, long-term care, inflation, and running out of retirement savings were not overriding concerns or risks.

The Current Generation's Retirement

Things are quite different today. People are now retiring as early as their 50s and, regardless of age, retirement can very realistically last 30 years or more due to increased life expectancies. The reality is more people are now living into their 90s and even 100s than ever before. Think about that for a moment. Your retirement distribution plan may need to last for as many years (or more) as you were in the workforce! Furthermore, a lot more of one's retirement assets are typically invested in the stock market these days. All of this subjects them to many of the risks discussed throughout this book.

In addition, stock market crashes, recessions, low interest rates, inflation, healthcare expenses are real concerns as people age. Future retirees also face the possibility of paying more taxes in the future than they do now, like property taxes, sales tax, and especially income taxes. Furthermore, due to increased life expectancies, retirees now require a plan to insure or budget for the possibility of having to pay for long-term care. Finally, one of the biggest concerns and financial risks most retirees now face is outliving their retirement assets and income (i.e., longevity risk).

You now have to think differently about how a very long retirement can impact and potentially put "stress" on your retirement assets that are supposed to sustain your cash flow throughout retirement. It is imperative that your retirement distribution phase be thoroughly planned out, even more so than your accumulation phase.

Where to Start

Where should you start when creating *your* ideal retirement plan? The answer is, start at the end. In other words, ask yourself what do you want to happen with your money after you're gone. For example, do you want to be sure to leave enough money for your spouse to continue his or her retirement comfortably?

Perhaps you want to leave money to your children or grandchildren or extended family, such as nieces, nephews, or cousins? How about a close friend? What about leaving money to charities or religious organizations? If so, do you want your beneficiaries to pay the least amount of income taxes (or estate taxes, if applicable) when they inherit your money?1 Perhaps you don't have any family or friends you can or even want to leave money to. If so, that's okay. The point is, regardless of your intended plans for your money when you leave this earth, this should definitely be addressed and discussed early in your retirement planning. Therefore, creating your ideal retirement plan with your desired or ideal *end* is actually a good way to *start*.

If your goal is to make sure you leave sufficient assets or a financial legacy to your beneficiaries or designate who inherits what, then you will want to establish the proper estate plan. This means properly listing your designated beneficiaries on your accounts and creating a will and/or the appropriate type of trust (for this, be sure to seek the professional guidance of an estate-planning attorney). Perhaps you will want to consider the use of life insurance in your plan as well. Life insurance is probably the best way to transfer money to your beneficiaries. That's because you can do it for *pennies on the dollar*. But don't just take my word for it—financial industry experts Ed Slott and Tom Hegna highly recommend using life insurance for retirement and estate-planning objectives. If you decide to utilize life insurance, you'll want to determine the appropriate type of life insurance policy and how the premiums will be paid. For instance, will premium payments come from savings, investments, or from your retirement accounts, such as your IRA or 401(k)? Any of the above are viable options.

It's Not Just How Much You Need, but How Much You Want

Next, you will want to determine how much you need… or better yet, how much you *want* for your retirement income. It is one thing to know how much you need, but it is another to know how much you want. I suggest focusing on the want.

After all, if you're going to retire, you may as well be able to enjoy it, right? Perhaps you'd like to travel often or simply go out to dinner with friends and family on a regular basis. Maybe you'd like a nicer new car. Of course, you'll want to plan for any anticipated large expenses during retirement, such as a child's wedding, or perhaps a second home.

Keep in mind, you may have certain expenses that eventually will go away in retirement. For example, you may retire with a mortgage but know that mortgage will be paid off within the next few years. Or perhaps you will be selling your house to downsize, and your next home will be paid for in cash. In either scenario, your expenses will likely go down as a result of no longer having that mortgage payment. Also, by downsizing or relocating to another state, you may have lower property taxes and maintenance costs and, depending on the state, no state income tax.

How, Where, and When to Access Your Retirement Funds to Receive Cash Flow

Once you determine how much you need and want in retirement, you then need to develop your distribution strategy. As you should now understand, this is much different from your accumulation strategy. You will need to determine from which of your retirement accounts to take your retirement income. For example, do you take it from your 401(k) or traditional or rollover IRAs first? Or do you continue to defer the taxes from those accounts as long as possible and instead take income withdrawals from your other accounts that are not your 401(k) or IRAs?

Perhaps you take your retirement income *pro rata* (proportionately). In other words, a pro rata percentage is withdrawn from each of your accounts to provide your retirement income such as from your IRA(s), 401(k) as well as nonretirement accounts—where income or realized gains on your savings and investments are taxed in the year earned, such as an individual or joint owned brokerage account. For example, if you need or want $40,000 a year in retirement income and have $1 million that is allocated as follows: $350,000 in your traditional IRA, $100,000 in your spouse's traditional IRA, $300,000 in your 401(k), and $250,000 in a nonretirement brokerage account, you can take a pro rata percentage from each of these accounts to generate $40,000.

If you have a Roth IRA or Roth 401(k) account, you probably want to defer withdrawals from these accounts as long as possible since this will help maximize the growth or earnings potential that's available tax-free for you and for your beneficiaries. Just remember, there can be many ways to go about this.

The next question is, where will you put your money when you retire to help you achieve your goals and objectives? There are many savings, investments and financial products to consider. Some of these include stocks, bonds, mutual funds, exchange-traded funds (ETFs), unit investment trusts (UITs), third-party money managers, and real estate investment trusts (REITs). Other financial products include private equity and private debt; fixed, variable, and fixed-index annuities; cash value life insurance; money markets; and certificates of deposit (CDs). Perhaps the appropriate savings and investment allocation for your retirement assets is a combination of all or most of the above options. Regardless, it's important to remember that you are now looking to create cash flow, not looking for rates of return.

Of course, your risk tolerance also needs to be factored into your decision. As I stated, people have different tolerances for risk. However, most retirees prefer less risk. In addition, you need to factor in your potential life expectancy (i.e., how long you expect to live). Obviously, you don't know exactly how long you will live. However, you can certainly make some reasonable assumptions. For example, if your parents are healthy, are in their 90s, and you are also healthy, then you should realistically plan to live into your 90s as well. Regardless of your family's historical life expectancy, I strongly suggest planning to live longer than you think you will. The last thing you'd want is to run out of retirement income because you lived longer than you had planned for and didn't account for that possibility in your retirement plan.

If you have a pension, you need to understand your available options. For example, can you take your pension as a lump sum or is a monthly annuity your only choice? If you can take a lump sum, is that the most appropriate option based on your objectives, needs, and risk tolerance? Where will you put the lump sum? Will you roll it over into an IRA to defer paying income taxes, or will you instead pay the taxes on it now and move the remaining after-tax funds into a nonretirement account? If your only option is a monthly annuity, what age will be ideal for you to start the annuity payments?

Regarding the inevitable fees, they are certainly relevant and important, but again, don't base your financial decisions on fees alone. Understand what it is that you will you be getting for those fees. Just considering low fee options doesn't guarantee more income. What good is it to pay a lower fee only to end up running out of money in retirement or having to take less income throughout retirement? Author, economist, and retirement expert Tom Hegna states it best: "I don't get to retire on low fees. I get to retire on the products that make the most and lose the least *after* fees!" Therefore, look at the big picture and try to see the forest, instead of just the trees.

Do You Have Enough to Retire?

Clients often ask me if they have enough money to retire. My response is that I first need to know two main things:

1. How much money do you currently have or plan to have at retirement?
2. How much income (i.e., cash flow) will you need or want during retirement?

This is why these answers are so important. Let's say you have a million dollars for retirement. If you need $40,000 a year of retirement income (excluding Social Security or a pension), then you are probably in a good position to retire. However, if you need $150,000 a year and have no monthly pension (perhaps only Social Security), then you probably haven't saved enough to retire just yet. Withdrawing $150,000 a year will require a very high withdrawal rate that is likely unsustainable and you run the risk of depleting your retirement account. And you now know what that means: no account value, no income! (Unless of course, you have an annuity that is providing you with guaranteed lifetime income.)
Your ideal retirement plan should be able to provide you with the following:

- Tax-advantaged retirement income (i.e., tax-free cash flow and access to your money)
- Growth of your retirement assets and retirement income to help keep pace with the rising costs that most retirees will face
- Appropriate insurance policies and coverages, including medical and long-term care, as well as life insurance that can help pay for the potential income and/or estate tax liabilities, replace depleted retirement assets, or to leave a financial legacy
- Noncorrelated and low volatility assets that are not fully subjected to all the risks of the stock or bond markets
- Assets consisting of both savings and investments (as you now know, savings and investments are *not* the same)
- Last and most important, reliable, preferably guaranteed lifetime income to ensure sufficient cash flow

Putting Your Retirement Plan Together

As you start getting closer to retirement, it's extremely important to review your *at-risk* investments, such as your stocks, bonds, mutual funds, real estate, etc. Then look to make the appropriate changes or adjustments. It's much better to do this sooner rather than later. Don't base your decision to make changes or not on how the stock market is doing or how well your investments are performing at that given point in time. By waiting, you could be caught off guard in the event of a sudden market correction or crash, as so many retirees and pre-retirees were in 2008. Depending on what type of investments you have, it may take years to recover. As of the writing of this book, real estate in some parts of the country still haven't gotten back to pre-2008 values. And remember what we explored earlier in this book—just getting back to even does not recoup your "lost earnings" during the down time.

For the above reasons, I usually suggest planning for and setting up your retirement distribution strategy at least five years prior to your planned retirement date. Ten years is even better. If you think ten years is too soon, remember the "lost decade" (2000-2009) when the S&P 500® index, with dividends reinvested, real rate of return was negative?[2] It's not just real estate that can stagnate. Truth is, it's never too soon. Therefore, you should realign your retirement accounts to their proper risk profile so you can avoid getting burned by the next market correction or crash.

It is also the time to start learning about and understanding the savings, investments, and financial products that are most appropriate for the retirement distribution phase and more specifically—that are right for you and your situation. In particular, the ones that will provide the amount of retirement cash flow you need and want. Remember, what you use to get *to* retirement may no longer be the most appropriate *during* retirement. Also, keep in mind, there are no good or bad investments or financial products; there are only appropriate or inappropriate investments or financial products.

In addition, look into how you can best maximize your retirement cash flow with the least amount of risk and tax consequences. There are many ways to accomplish this. Throughout this book, I provide you with some general ideas and strategies to help get you thinking. Remember, there is not just one way to accomplish this. You need to determine what is most appropriate for you to help meet your financial objectives. In retirement, it's no longer just about growth and asset allocation. It's now about creating cash flow and utilizing the financial products available to help maximize it with the least amount of risk.

Think about it, do you really want to be scrambling to learn all of this right before you're about to retire? Not likely, right? All that will do is add unnecessary anxiety and stress. This is certainly not what you should have to be dealing with during what should be an exciting new chapter in your life. The plan should be *cruising*, not scrambling, into retirement.

Longevity Risk
"The volatility of longevity is on the same order of magnitude as the stock market. You need a risk management strategy for both."
—Dr. Moshe Milevsky

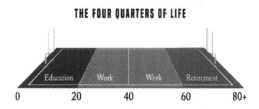

THE FOUR QUARTERS OF LIFE

I often say that our lives are like a football game, meaning they can be segmented into quarters. For example, the first quarter represents our years in school. The second and third quarters represent our years in the workforce. The fourth quarter represents our retirement. However, now that we are living longer, and often retiring earlier, many of us are now going into overtime and for some, double overtime in retirement. Which leads us to another risk retirees now face: longevity risk.

The fact is, you can't have an ideal retirement plan without addressing longevity risk. Longevity risk is the *very real* risk of outliving your retirement assets and income. Investments, such as mutual funds, target date funds, or company stock, often available in a 401(k), are not designed to protect you against longevity risk. Therefore, as you get closer to retirement, you will want to seek out ways to not only maximize your retirement cash flow but do so on a reliable and even guaranteed basis to protect yourself from longevity risk. These ways can consist of pensions (if applicable), Social Security, and annuities. In fact, according to Dr. Wade Pfau, professor of retirement income at The American College of Financial Services, "By combining an income annuity and stocks, you get the most efficient outcome… Annuities are better suited than stocks for protecting against longevity risk and investment volatility. Partial annuitization of a portfolio stabilizes the legacy value of the assets."

The following are other things to consider.

Pay Taxes Now or Pay Taxes Later?

In general, I personally believe it's better to pay taxes on the seed (the seed is the contribution toward saving and investing) and not on the harvest (the harvest is the retirement income withdrawals). Now, I want to emphasize that I said *in general*, because as I have been saying throughout this book, everyone's situation is different. There is no one-size-fits-all.

However, by paying tax on the seed, you know exactly what the tax rate is on that income. Furthermore, it's on a small amount compared to the likely large amount you will withdraw later on during retirement. Also, as previously discussed, where do you believe income tax rates will be in the future? No one really knows, but there is a very strong case as of the writing of this book that they could be going up in the future—after all, our national debt and the cost of our various government programs, such as Social Security and Medicare, are only increasing. At some point, these financial obligations will need to be addressed. Regardless, the reality is that no one knows the economic, market, or political conditions that will exist in the future. Therefore, why gamble and take the risk that you will end up paying taxes at a higher rate when you retire?

Let's look at this another way. Would you accept a loan from a bank or credit union today without knowing the interest rate until sometime in the future—like when the loan is paid off? Furthermore, what if the chances were likely that the interest rate would be higher? Would you agree to such terms? I'm sure not. But that's exactly what you're doing when you defer taxes now in your retirement accounts and "accept the terms" that you will pay the taxes at future rates when you start to take your retirement income withdrawals.

If income tax rates do increase (whether federal, state, or both), you would then need to increase the amount you withdraw just to cover your increased tax liability in order to continue to receive the same after-tax income or cash flow. For example, if you have $1.2 million in retirement assets and withdrawing 5 percent, this results in a gross or pre-tax monthly cash flow of $5,000 (5 percent of $1.2 million equals $60,000 per year, which is $5,000 per month). If you are in a 20 percent tax bracket, this will leave you with $4,000 after-tax per month. (Whether this 20 percent rate consists of federal and/or state income taxes is not relevant for this example.) However, if your income tax rate increases from 20 to 25 percent, in order to maintain the same after-tax cash flow of $4,000, you will have to increase your gross (pre-tax) withdrawal from $5,000 to $5,334. That increase of $334 per month is just to pay the additional income tax; it's not available to spend or continue to save or invest. Furthermore, this action also increases your withdrawal percentage rate. And keep in mind, the federal and/or state income tax rates could very well continue to increase even further (not to mention, local or property taxes).

Likewise, the impact of inflation may force you to increase your withdrawals too. Inflation is often referred to as a "hidden tax" because you don't pay it or owe it to the government—but it does reduce the purchasing power of your spendable income or cash flow requiring you to increase your withdrawals just to maintain your standard of living.

All these factors would require increased withdrawals, which effectively increases your withdrawal percentage rate and therefore increases your risk of depleting your retirement funds.

What if your retirement assets are invested in the stock market? If you have to eventually increase your withdrawals to account for higher taxes and/or the impact of inflation, this can further subject you to both sequence of returns and market volatility risk. Or, what if your retirement assets are held in interest-earning accounts (e.g., a money market, CD, bond mutual fund, or fixed annuity)? Increasing the withdrawals from these accounts can put you at risk of eventually depleting them as well if the withdrawal rate is higher than the interest you are earning. Remember, no account value means no income (unless of course, you are using an annuity with a guaranteed lifetime income benefit rider).

Now, let's look at another aspect of this situation. When you turn age 70½ and have retirement accounts such as IRAs or 401(k)s (Roth IRAs are excluded), you will have required minimum distributions (RMDs) to contend with. RMDs are mandatory distributions each year from qualified retirement accounts, such as a 401(k), or a traditional or rollover IRA. The minimum amount that must be withdrawn each year is based on the prior calendar-year-end account values from *all* of your retirement accounts (excluding Roth IRAs) and using the IRS (Internal Revenue Service) Uniform Lifetime Table to calculate the required minimum distribution for that year. It starts out somewhat low (currently 3.65 percent) and increases each year as you get older. This mandatory withdrawal results in taxable income to you. The way our current tax system works, your regular taxable retirement income and withdrawals, plus your RMDs, could actually bump you into the *next higher* tax bracket.

Also, the result of this additional taxable income could adversely impact other things such as having your Social Security benefits being taxed (or having more of it taxed), your Medicare premiums increased, or your property taxes increased due to the loss of the senior freeze exemption. Having to increase your taxable income for RMDs or to pay for these increasing expenses as a result of your RMDs could put you into the higher tax bracket that you thought you'd avoid in retirement.

Don't be caught off-guard. Plan for the worst-case scenario. For example, as I stated in Chapter 1 on life insurance, plan as if the life insurance is going to be needed, by obtaining the maximum coverage, and then hope that it isn't. Therefore, you should definitely plan for higher taxes and higher expenses in the future. This is why both advanced planning and creating a tax-free retirement cash flow strategy are so important.

Even if you are currently working, in the highest tax bracket, and expect to live off less income in retirement (likely putting you in a lower tax bracket), there is still a very compelling reason why you should still accumulate some after-tax and/or tax-free cash flow assets for retirement as well—control and flexibility. For example, if you need a one-time withdrawal to purchase a car, instead of having to take an additional withdrawal that would be taxable (which you've now seen can have various consequences), you could take that withdrawal from an account that wouldn't incur income taxes (e.g., a Roth IRA or cash value life insurance) and therefore avoid going into a higher tax bracket. This plan also reduces your chances of paying more for other things, such as Medicare or property taxes.

Remember, if all or even most of your retirement income is subject to income taxes when withdrawn, there is a strong possibility that it could end up having an unfavorable effect on your cash flow. The issue and concern is that these unforeseen or unplanned for situations can adversely impact your retirement strategy.

Roth IRA and Roth 401(k) Accounts Can Provide
Tax-Free Retirement Cash Flow

Whether you have been saving and investing for many years or are just starting out, you should consider the benefits of a Roth IRA or, if available, a Roth 401(k) or 403(b) through your retirement plan at work. Also, you should consider Roth IRA conversions. A Roth IRA conversion is when you move money from your traditional or rollover IRA into a Roth IRA. The pre-tax contributions plus earnings that you convert are subject to income taxes. However, it's generally not subject to the 10 percent early distribution penalty if you are under age 59½ and pay the income taxes with funds outside of the IRA account. Currently, there is no longer an income cap to convert from a traditional IRA to a Roth IRA; however, there may be other tax implications when doing so. Therefore, you should consult with a tax advisor or CPA first. If you do consider converting your traditional or rollover IRA to a Roth IRA, remember that it doesn't have to be an *all or nothing* conversion. You can (and it's probably best) convert your IRA to a Roth IRA over a period of time. This can help minimize the tax impact compared to doing it all at once.

All your cash flow doesn't necessarily have to be 100 percent tax-free. The reality is, you'll likely have at least some of your retirement assets in accounts that are taxable when withdrawn. This could be a pension, company-match contributions in a 401(k), or your elected pre-tax 401(k) contributions. However, by building up accounts that can be accessed tax-free, you'll create a much more controlled, flexible, and tax-efficient retirement distribution plan. Don't forget high cash value life insurance. This is another prudent strategy to provide yourself with tax-free cash flow.

The Known and Unknown Expenses of Medical and Long-Term Care

An example of a known expense is, at least initially, medical insurance. As you approach retirement, you should determine what your medical expense outlay during retirement will likely be. Generally, known expenses within this realm include premiums, deductibles, copays, and the cost of medications. Also, you should decide whether or not to purchase dental or eye care insurance. In addition, you may already have certain ongoing expenses, like chiropractic treatment, that you know will continue into retirement, so remember to account for these too. These are expenses that you will continue to be paying for in retirement; therefore, you must factor them into your monthly cash flow budget.

An example of an unknown expense would be some sort of financial emergency that arises, out-of-pocket costs above your deductible due to a car accident, or incurring medical expenses not covered by insurance. They are unknown expenses because you don't know if they will actually occur nor what they will cost. However, the idea is to plan ahead; like the "rainy day fund" you may have already had for years. One way to approach this is to talk to older family members or people you know and ask them what unexpected expenses they have experienced in retirement. This may give you ideas that you wouldn't have thought of otherwise.

Another example of an unknown expense is long-term care. This expense could be anywhere from tens of thousands of dollars to literally hundreds of thousands of dollars. Or it could be zero, assuming you never need long-term care and never purchased a long-term care policy. This can be a catch-22 because you don't know whether you will ever need long-term care. Many people know that long-term care can be outrageously expensive. But the decision to purchase long-term care insurance is often a conflict for many because it is perceived as a lot of money being spent on premiums to insure against a risk that may never occur. But, that is the whole purpose of insurance—to insure a risk that can potentially be very costly or catastrophic. Retirement does not mean you can be penny wise and dollar foolish. You should seriously look to include some sort of funding for potential long-term care needs. This could include allocating funds to a separate savings or investment account and/or funds to pay for a long-term care insurance policy. A long-term care insurance policy can at least help to outsource some of that risk.

Another way to outsource the risk of potential long-term care expenses is to use one of the asset-based (or hybrid) long-term care insurance products available. This involves an annuity or a life insurance policy with a long-term care benefit feature or rider. The benefit of these types of products is that you can generally make just one premium payment (i.e., single lump sum payment) or make a series of premium payments for a select number of years (e.g., 5 years). In addition, they are guaranteed to never have a rate increase that would result in additional premiums being required or a decrease in benefits. In the event you never need long-term care, the annuity or life insurance policy will provide a death benefit (tax-free, if life insurance) to your named beneficiaries when you pass away. Also, if you no longer want or feel the need for the coverage for any reason, or if you need access to the cash value in the annuity or life insurance policy, you can generally cancel and have the remaining amount of cash surrender value paid out to you.[3] The cash surrender amount will depend upon various factors. However, keep in mind, this will eliminate your coverage.

These asset-based long-term care policies can be a prudent way to help insure against this potential costly expense. And, if you never need long-term care, you didn't "waste the premiums" so to speak. The most important takeaway here is that, statistically speaking, there is a good chance you (and if married, your spouse) will need some type of long-term care at some point. The likelihood of this happening increases the longer you live. Without proper long-term care insurance coverage, you run the risk that long-term care costs may deplete your retirement savings and income. This risk is further magnified if you are married. You certainly don't want to leave your spouse with nothing because all your retirement assets were spent to pay for your long-term care needs. Therefore, you really need to consider this in your retirement plan. In fact, it's important to consider all of your available options to help protect yourself, your spouse, your children, etc.

Of course, you always have the option to self-insure. This means you take on 100 percent of the risk of paying for potential long-term care expenses yourself. But why take on all the risk when you can simply leverage some of that "rainy day fund," for example, to create 2–5 times the available funds that can be used to provide coverage for a possible long-term care event? Therefore, I suggest the prudent strategy is to outsource at least some of the risk by purchasing some type of long-term care policy and then perhaps self-insure the rest of the risk. You can self-insure by planning to use available cash flow or setting aside some savings or retirement assets. Just be sure to factor this in ahead of time as you are creating your ideal retirement plan.

Need a Loan or Mortgage in Retirement?

Have you ever tried qualifying for a loan or mortgage with no income, or know someone who has tried? You can't do it. At the very least, it's certainly difficult. Banks won't lend without seeing income. You could literally have millions of dollars at the bank, in your retirement accounts, etc. and you likely still won't qualify. Seems crazy, right? But it's true for the most part. Banks usually want to see that you have an income stream (i.e., cash flow) each and every month. Many retirees who try to refinance or take out a mortgage (e.g., to downsize or for a winter home) are surprised that they can't qualify, even with millions in liquid (i.e., accessible) retirement assets. Therefore, setting up your retirement plan to provide reliable (better yet, guaranteed) cash flow will absolutely put you in a much better position to help qualify for that loan or mortgage.

Liquidity of Your Assets versus Cash Flow from Your Assets

In Chapter 3, I explained why liquidity is not an investor's friend. I will now explain why it's not a retiree's friend either.

Much of the financial services industry, along with many of the media pundits, constantly preach that retirees must maintain liquidity of their assets—which is really their way of saying to invest their assets in the stock market. This is simply misguided advice. Liquidity of assets should not be the main priority in retirement. Creating reliable and even guaranteed cash flow should be the main priority of every retiree.

The ideal retirement plan will be able to provide for both sufficient cash flow and adequate liquidity. However, keep in mind, a retiree certainly doesn't require liquidity from the assets that are used to generate their retirement cash flow. In fact, that's the last thing they need. If they liquidate assets from the accounts that are providing them retirement cash flow, they most likely will receive less cash flow in the future. They will be forced to take a "pay cut" or risk eventually depleting the account. A retiree should not be placed in this situation simply because of the misconception that you need liquidity for all your assets.

Instead, a retiree's liquidity needs should come from financial products held in a separate account and that are not needed for generating cash flow. These are the accounts where you will go to help pay for any "one-off" expenses (e.g., paying off a debt, replacing a furnace, etc.), and include a savings account, money market, stock portfolio, mutual funds, fixed annuity, cash value life insurance, etc.

Remember, financial products used for liquidity are no more important than financial products designed for cash flow, even if the result is a lack of liquidity. That's because a retiree can usually find an alternative such as making installment payments on a medical bill if they can't pay in full. However, there is no alternative around a lack of cash flow. Therefore, cash flow needs to be the priority—not liquidity. Of course, it would be nice to have both. But given the choice, cash flow is far more important. Not only do retirees need to think this way, the financial services industry would better serve retirees by advising them to think this way as well.

You should be thinking in terms of how much of your retirement assets can be designated to provide reliable and guaranteed cash flow while still maintaining enough assets for potential liquidity needs. Unfortunately, most people think how few assets can be designated to provide reliable and guaranteed cash flow simply to maintain liquidity. This is not a prudent way to think. In fact, by simply maximizing your cash flow, you can create excess cash flow, which can then be allocated to a separate account that is now available to provide for any liquidity needs.

Social Security

Let's explore the role of Social Security in helping to create your ideal retirement plan. There are many different opinions on when to start Social Security. You will often hear the recommendation to defer your Social Security benefits for as long as possible. The reason is, the longer you wait, the higher your monthly benefit will be. Currently, you can maximize your benefits by deferring until age 70. After that, your benefit no longer increases by waiting. However, regardless of when you start, there is still the potential for cost-of-living increases based on the consumer price index (CPI). As I have emphasized throughout this book, don't rely on generalizations, rules of thumb, or doing what "everyone else" is doing. There are many factors in determining when it's most appropriate for *you* to start taking Social Security benefits. First, if you need the monthly income when you retire in order to get by (i.e., pay your monthly bills), then it's a no-brainer, in that case, you pretty much have to start collecting Social Security, assuming you are at the minimum age to collect, which is currently 62. Other factors to consider are whether you are single or married, the amount of cash flow you can generate from your retirement savings to meet your current income needs or wants, and your estimated life expectancy.

You also need to determine whether you should use your Social Security payments for existing living expenses, put them into savings (perhaps to build an emergency fund), or invest them. If you don't need the income for your monthly expenses and are concerned that you may pass away before collecting, then you may want to consider starting your benefit as soon as you are eligible. You can therefore save or invest it to leave a financial legacy eventually.

In the case of leaving a financial legacy, you could consider using your Social Security benefits to pay premiums for a life insurance policy. As mentioned earlier, this is a great strategy to use cash flow (whether it's Social Security or any other cash flow) that's not needed for living expenses to "leverage" what you leave to your beneficiaries. Also, by having a life insurance policy, you can use the death benefit proceeds to replace those lost Social Security benefits for your spouse or other beneficiaries once you pass away. Furthermore, as mentioned earlier in this chapter, you could possibly add a long-term care rider to the life insurance policy. This can be a very prudent and cost-effective method of insuring the risk of long-term care expenses for you and your spouse.

One of the other key factors I often see overlooked in determining when you should start Social Security is understanding the impact it can have on the overall value of your retirement assets or net worth. For example, if you defer your Social Security, you will have to "support" your standard of living solely from your retirement assets (unless you also have a pension to cover the difference, but then you must decide whether or not to defer collecting on that too). Doing so could reduce the value of your retirement assets in the future for you, your spouse, or your beneficiaries—or just simply preventing those assets from growing depending, of course, on exactly how or where you have your retirement assets saved or invested and how much you need to withdraw. For example, if you're invested in the stock and bond markets and using a systematic withdrawal, this withdrawal strategy could reduce your account value if the markets drop and/or you withdraw at too high of a withdrawal rate, resulting in the possibility of having to lower the amount of your retirement income (i.e., cash flow) at some point, or worse, depleting your account altogether and therefore having no retirement income available from your retirement assets. You may then be left with only Social Security (or perhaps your pension too), a position you most likely do not want to be in.

You might think this is not a real concern since you could eventually offset the potential need to lower your retirement income by taking your Social Security benefit at a later time, which would result in a higher monthly benefit. This scenario could possibly make you "whole" again. This is possible and should be considered when looking into your options. However, you still need to factor in the possibility of needing *more*, not *less*, income in the future for any unknown expenses (e.g., long-term care).

If your ideal retirement plan includes leaving as much as possible to your beneficiaries, then deferring Social Security may not be the most appropriate strategy either. It's important to understand that once you pass away, your Social Security benefit will stop. If you are married, your surviving spouse[4] will only receive the higher of each of your two benefits, not both. This is important to plan for because a spouse's death always results in a reduction of the combined Social Security benefits to the surviving spouse. However, your retirement accounts would still be available for your spouse, children, or other beneficiaries.

Once you learn and understand all the pros and cons, you can then make a more informed decision on when to start Social Security based on your own personal objectives.

Using Annuities to Provide Guaranteed Cash Flow for Life

As you have seen so far, there are various types of annuities available to provide guaranteed lifetime income. There are immediate annuities, which can pay a fixed-level monthly income or an increasing monthly income. While your initial income starts out lower with an increasing monthly payout than a fixed-level income payout, over time the increasing income annuity can eventually pay out more each month than the fixed-level option.

Annuities can offer a cash refund option. If you decide to cash out of the annuity and the full amount of your premium deposit has yet to be completely distributed, you can generally receive a discounted (i.e., present value) amount of the undistributed premium back in a lump sum payment. This option is also available to your beneficiaries.

In addition, some annuities offer a life-with-period-certain payout. With this option, payments are for life, however, should you pass away within a certain period, the payments will continue to pay out for the remaining period-certain to your named beneficiaries. For example, if the annuity is a life-with-10-year-period-certain payout and you pass away in year 6, your beneficiaries will continue to receive the payout for 4 more years. After that, the payout stops. Regardless of whether the annuity offers a cash refund or a life-with-period-certain, it will pay out to *you* for as long as you live.

Then there are both variable annuities and fixed-index annuities with guaranteed lifetime income benefit riders (these riders usually come with an additional fee). These types of annuities were discussed in Chapter 6.

Any of these types of annuities will most likely allow you to take withdrawals at a higher withdrawal rate than what you could reasonably expect from other savings and investments options, such as what Wall Street, the big brand-name and discount brokerage firms, and media pundits would suggest. However, unlike what they suggest, you would not run the risk of losing that income if the account value should ever deplete to zero. The withdrawal rates on annuities vary but are generally anywhere from 4–7 percent. (Some immediate annuities and deferred income annuities may be even higher, depending on age and other factors.) This is clearly higher than the "supposed" safe, systematic withdrawal rate of 3 percent or less.

The payout rates on variable and fixed-index annuities are usually based on age and on a single-life or joint-life payout. For example, a single person age 65 may have a guaranteed lifetime withdrawal rate of 5.5 percent. If this person is married, and the spouse is the same age, and they elect the joint-life payout, then the guaranteed lifetime withdrawal rate may be slightly lower—say, 5 percent.

Think about this—the recommended retirement income withdrawal rate from investments, such as mutual funds, is around 3 percent (or less). Yet, you still run the risk of depleting the account value to zero. And you should now know what happens: you no longer will receive income from that account. Instead, you can choose an annuity with a guaranteed lifetime income benefit rider, with perhaps a 5 percent withdrawal rate, and eliminate the risk of running out of money. Not only does the annuity guarantee your income, but it can provide anywhere from 30–70 percent more income than any stock or mutual fund portfolio. Furthermore, just think of how much more income the annuity could provide compared to any fixed account options available, such as a CD, money market, bond, or bond mutual fund.

Let's look at an example. Let's say you have $1 million in your 401(k) at retirement. You saved long and hard for many years and you are now officially a millionaire. (I know, that doesn't quite seem to mean the same as it once did.)

Congratulations! But, what does that get you in retirement?

If you put that $1 million into a certificate of deposit (CD) at the bank or credit union at, say, 1 percent, it would provide you with $833 in monthly cash flow. Not very exciting. (This is just an example—I hope you'd never put a million dollars into a 1 percent CD in order to generate retirement income.) Of course, that's *pre-tax* monthly cash flow (assuming your retirement assets consisted of pre-tax dollars, as most do), so your actual spendable income would be less. The exact amount would be based on your tax bracket.

Now, let's say you instead invested the $1 million in the stock market and used the financial services industry's recommended "safe" withdrawal rate of 2.8 percent. This would provide you with $2,333 in pre-tax cash flow. Again, not very exciting. That doesn't even cover a mortgage payment and property taxes in many cities. However, if you used an annuity (and depending on your age and whether you use single- or joint-lifetime income or payout options), you could receive $3,333 to $5,000 (maybe even more) in pre-tax cash flow per month. Furthermore, that cash flow is guaranteed.

Which of the above cash flow scenarios would you rather have? I think the choice is quite obvious, don't you? Remember, this is an example. You certainly wouldn't put all of your retirement assets into an annuity. In fact, as I've stated, you shouldn't put all your retirement assets into any one type of investment or financial product. It's always wise to diversify among various types of financial products.

Here is a second example, addressing it from an *income-first* perspective (i.e., starting with your targeted income goal and then working backward to determine how your assets need to be allocated to generate the income need or want). Let's say you want $50,000 in annual retirement cash flow above and beyond Social Security or any pension benefits. How much do you need from your retirement assets to generate $50,000 a year? If you wanted to live off the interest alone, and assuming interest rates are at 2 percent, you would need $2.5 million in retirement assets. That's a lot to have to save for a $50,000-a-year retirement income. However, if you could generate a 5 percent withdrawal rate using an annuity, you would only need to accumulate $1 million. That changes things, doesn't it? That's a lot less you have to save—and potentially the difference between an enjoyable retirement or just getting by. If you look at it this way, you may even be ready to retire sooner than you thought.

Now, let's look at a third example. You have accumulated $1 million for retirement at age 65. You need $40,000 a year in retirement income, excluding Social Security. If you put $800,000 into an annuity paying a 5 percent guaranteed lifetime distribution rate, it would generate the $40,000 annual income, guaranteed for life, that you need to live comfortably. That would leave you with $200,000 that can remain liquid and earn interest and/or dividends or even be invested for potential growth. Some of it could even go toward an asset-based long-term care insurance policy. Even if that $200,000 generated only 3 percent, that's an additional $6,000 a year or $500 per month of retirement income. This additional income could allow you to actually do all those extras you didn't think you could afford to do.

As Dr. Wade Pfau states:

> "To build an efficient retirement strategy, you need to integrate both stocks and an annuity into the plan. For essential spending, you don't want to be exposed just to the stock market; you want to have something more secure in place. For discretionary expenses, that's where you can be invested in stocks and be more aggressive."

Something else to consider: do you really want to manage your investments during retirement? Keep in mind, at some point in the future, you may not even have the mental capacity to do so, even if you wanted to. Furthermore, do you really want someone who works for Wall Street, a big brand-name firm, or a discount brokerage firm to be managing your retirement assets at a time when you may not fully understand what is going on or what they may be recommending as you age? Even if you have a long-time, trusted financial advisor at one of those firms, what happens if he or she retires or simply leaves the industry for whatever reason? At least with an annuity that provides guaranteed lifetime income, those types of concerns go away, or at the very least, become less of a concern.

Annuities can also make for a happier retirement. Willis Towers Watson, a leading global professional services company, conducted a 2012 study, "Annuities and Retirement Happiness,"[5] and here is what they found: "Annuities protect retirees from longevity risk and establish a floor of income—beyond the modest annuity paid by Social Security—safe from investment losses." In addition, they cited a study from 2003 that found "retirees with a higher percentage of annuitized income were happier on a cross-sectional basis and maintained higher levels of satisfaction over time than their less annuitized counterparts." Who doesn't want to be happier and more satisfied in retirement, especially when studies like this show that it can help be achieved with something as simple and as easily accessible as including annuities into your retirement plan? Therefore, look to find the right type or types of annuities can that work best for your situation. An independent financial advisor who understands the importance of guaranteed lifetime income can be of great help to you with this.

Now, if your pension and/or Social Security, both of which also provide guaranteed lifetime income, provide you with sufficient retirement income, then the need for annuities for guaranteed lifetime income is less essential. However, if this is not case, then these types of retirement income annuities can be extremely beneficial not only to secure your retirement income, regardless of how long you live, but also provide you with peace of mind. How much is peace of mind worth to you?

●　　●　　●　　●　　●

Strategies to Create Cash Flow During Retirement

The following strategies can be used to create cash flow during retirement. They are by no means an actual plan or personal recommendations. The fact is, there are just too many missing details and other factors to consider for anyone to simply adopt these strategies "as is." Remember, everyone's situation is different. I present these just to get you thinking and to make you aware of strategies you may not have considered. That's the role of a true fiduciary. In addition, be sure you have a rationale for why your money is allocated to a specific investment or financial product. In other words, ask yourself what is the benefit and value you are receiving by putting your retirement assets into, for example, mutual funds, a stock portfolio, a fixed annuity, or a variable annuity with a guaranteed lifetime income benefit rider. Remember, it's about what can work best for you, which is why I suggest seeking the advice of an independent financial advisor to prepare a plan tailored to your own specific situation.

Strategy 1
Combining a Systematic Withdrawal Strategy
with Guaranteed Lifetime Cash Flow

Take your retirement income withdrawals proportionately across all your retirement assets. For example, a pro rata withdrawal from your no-risk accounts, (e.g., a money market) and your at-risk accounts (e.g., mutual funds). Yes, this is a systematic withdrawal strategy and I have been warning you of its risks. However, if you insist on this type of strategy, here are some ways to help mitigate the risk of outliving your retirement income if your assets deplete to zero or if you have to reduce the amount you withdraw in order to prevent the account from depleting to zero.

When implementing a systematic withdrawal strategy, you should strongly consider deferring your pension and/or Social Security to maximize those monthly benefits. In addition, you should also consider placing some of your retirement assets into an annuity with a guaranteed lifetime income benefit rider and then defer withdrawals so that it can provide a higher income withdrawal base in the future. This could allow you to more confidently withdraw from your retirement assets and still have the peace of mind of knowing you have those guaranteed income sources available as a backup later in retirement.

Strategy 2
Combining a High Initial Systematic Withdrawal Strategy
with the Protection of Guaranteed Lifetime Cash Flow

This is somewhat like Strategy 1, except this one involves taking a lot more retirement income now with the assumption that you'll need or want less later in retirement or if you don't believe you will have a long life expectancy (i.e., longevity risk is not a real concern).

If you think you'll need or want more retirement income during your initial retirement years (e.g., so you can travel often) and then less later on, you could start with a much higher systematic withdrawal rate such as 6 or 7 percent, for example. Of course, this is much higher than the current suggested sustainable withdrawal rate of 3 percent or less, but it will at least allow you to spend more earlier in retirement when you are able to and want to with the assumption that you will eventually spend less later.

To help protect yourself from running out of retirement income with this much riskier withdrawal strategy—just as in Strategy 1—you should definitely consider deferring your Social Security (and pension, if you have one) and also placing some of your assets into annuities that can provide guaranteed growth *and* guaranteed lifetime income withdrawals. This can help eliminate the risk and concern if you deplete your assets—and as a result, the income from those assets—later in retirement. This is certainly a strategy that requires thorough planning and thought before putting into action. Keep in mind, if you are married or would like to leave a financial legacy, neither Strategy 1 or 2 is a prudent option.

Strategy 3
The Bucket or Time Segmentation Strategy

Divide your retirement assets into different accounts, with one account specifically designated for generating immediate cash flow while the other accounts are designated for deferral of cash flow and growth. This is often referred to as the "bucket" or "time segmentation" strategy. The objective is to withdraw your retirement income from one designated account that's safe, like a money market for example, over a short period of time, such as 3 to 5 years. This would be referred to as bucket 1 or segment 1. Once that account is about to deplete, you move assets from a second account (i.e., bucket 2 or segment 2) that has likely earned more money than the bucket 1 or segment 1 account. Since you weren't taking any withdrawals for those 3 to 5 years from the bucket 2 account, it doesn't require as much liquidity. It just requires safety of principal. This bucket 2 account could be a CD, short-term bond, or fixed annuity. You can then put the balance of your retirement assets into a third account or accounts (i.e., bucket 3 or segment 3) that can potentially provide for higher growth, such as stocks, mutual funds, unit investment trusts (UITs), variable annuities, etc. You may even be able to designate funds to a fourth bucket (i.e., bucket 4 or segment 4). This bucket or segment is typically used for legacy planning (i.e., assets you plan to leave to your designated beneficiaries) or for potential long-term care.

This strategy was more ideal back when interest rates on fixed accounts were higher. However, with interest rates currently at historical lows (as of 2018), you must increase the amount funded into the accounts of the first two buckets or segments in order to withdraw the equivalent cash flow. This means that you may have less funds available to be allocated to the later buckets or segments for growth. With this spend-down strategy, the lower interest rates may not make that much of a difference. However, don't just make that assumption. I'd suggest running an analysis to check how these low interest rates could impact you if you are considering using the bucket or time segmentation as a retirement distribution strategy.

Remember, you can't or shouldn't rely on the stock market to make up the difference. That's because if you're investing your long-term money in stocks or mutual funds, there is no guarantee you will get the growth rates required to maintain your desired cash flow throughout retirement. Furthermore, you run the risk that the stocks or mutual funds don't grow at all or worse, lose value. That's precisely why you need to consider guaranteed lifetime income strategies for at least part of your retirement assets. In fact, this is where you may want to consider using a variable annuity with a guaranteed lifetime income benefit rider that can provide growth, via annual credits or roll-ups, to your income withdrawal base, as discussed in Chapter 6.

Be sure to crunch the numbers and look at various scenarios in order to see how these projections might play out. This again, is where working with an independent financial advisor would be a great help.

Strategy 4
Guaranteed Lifetime Cash Flow to Cover Your Basic Living Expenses

Contribute sufficient retirement assets to guaranteed lifetime income annuities in order to cover your basic necessities or living expenses, such as your mortgage, utilities, and food. Then place the balance of your retirement assets into savings and investments, such as the ones mentioned in Chapter 5, to generate additional cash flow. This additional cash flow can then be used to pay for your discretionary expenses, such as travel and entertainment.

Strategy 5
Increasing Guaranteed Lifetime Cash Flow

Contribute to an increasing or inflation-adjusted immediate income annuity. This type of annuity provides cash flow that increases by a certain percentage every year in addition to providing guaranteed lifetime income. The income from this type of annuity will start out lower than a fixed-level income annuity but, over time, will eventually increase to a higher income payout. In the meantime, you could cover any shortfall in your desired income by saving or investing your other retirement assets so they can generate the additional cash flow required. Again, refer back to Chapter 5 for options.

You can also consider purchasing a variable or fixed-index annuity with a guaranteed lifetime income benefit rider that provides increasing income during the withdrawal or distribution phase. With these types of annuities, the initial withdrawal percentage rate is based on age and therefore the initial amount of the withdrawal isn't automatically reduced as it is with an inflation-adjusted immediate annuity.

Strategy 6
Combining Taxable and Tax-Free Retirement Cash Flow

Rather than just taking your retirement cash flow from your pre-tax IRA or 401(k) accounts that would be 100 percent taxable, consider taking your retirement cash flow from a combination of your pre-tax IRA or 401(k) accounts and your Roth IRA, Roth 401(k), cash value life insurance, and/or nonretirement accounts (e.g., individual or joint owned brokerage accounts). Here is an example. If you need or want $50,000 a year in after-tax retirement cash flow, you could withdraw $30,000 after-tax from your pre-tax IRA or 401(k) accounts and then withdraw $20,000 from your tax-free accounts. With this strategy, you only pay taxes on the pre-tax cash flow and not on the total cash flow. This strategy can help minimize your taxes, yet still allow you to withdraw the desired amount of cash flow you want.

Strategy 7
Tax-Free Retirement Cash Flow

This strategy requires advanced planning. With this strategy, you should maximize your Roth IRA and, if available, your Roth 401(k) contributions (up to the allowable annual limits) and/or convert your traditional or rollover IRA to a Roth IRA. Also, consider high cash value life insurance (as the wealthy do). This strategy will provide you with retirement cash flow that's tax-free. In fact, with proper planning, you could possibly get yourself into the lowest tax brackets without having to live off less income in retirement to do so. Wouldn't that be great? By starting early and with the proper planning and financial guidance, this can be a very obtainable goal. In fact, it's one of my personal retirement planning goals.

●   ●   ●   ●   ●

Strategies During Retirement to Help Preserve or Maximize Your Estate

If you would like to leave a financial legacy or minimize the potential income or estate taxes your beneficiaries may have to pay, then the following strategies may be appropriate and therefore should be considered. Again, these aren't specific recommendations. These are just ideas to get you thinking. Seek the advice of financial professionals, such as an estate-planning attorney, a CPA, and an independent financial advisor.

Strategy 8
Maximizing Your Guaranteed Lifetime Cash Flow to Purchase a Cash Value Life Insurance Policy

Place enough of your retirement assets into various types of annuities that not only provide guaranteed lifetime income but will also help to maximize your retirement cash flow. Take the excess income from the annuities that you aren't spending each month to purchase a cash value life insurance policy (i.e., permanent life insurance). With this strategy, you don't have to worry about running out of money because of the guaranteed lifetime income from the annuities. Then, when you pass away, the death benefit from the life insurance policy will pay out, tax-free, to your named beneficiaries to help to replenish any depletion of your retirement assets (or perhaps, increase your assets) so you can leave a financial legacy. The balance of your retirement assets can then be invested to pay for discretionary spending or to provide for other liquidity needs.

Here is an example. Let's say you have $1 million in retirement assets. We will assume you will need $30,000 a year (pre-tax) above what you'll receive from your Social Security benefit. You could put $700,000 into an annuity that pays a guaranteed lifetime income withdrawal amount of $38,500 a year assuming a 5.5 percent withdrawal rate. (Keep in mind, this is assumed to be taxable income, so your net after-tax spendable income will be less based on your tax bracket.) The $8,500 excess (less, applicable income taxes) can go to fund a cash value life insurance policy while the remaining $300,000 of retirement assets can be allocated to other savings and investments.

Strategy 9
Use Your Social Security Benefit
to Purchase a Cash Value Life Insurance Policy

A popular approach, as discussed earlier, is to defer Social Security for as long as you can. Again, this may or may not be your best option. There are a lot of things to consider given all the variables in each individual's or family's circumstances. The truth is, no one really knows with 100 percent certainty, what is the right or best option for any particular person—this can only be determined in hindsight.

That said, instead of deferring Social Security, you could start collecting as soon as you are eligible (currently age 62) and use the monthly benefit to purchase a cash value life insurance policy. You can set this up to have premiums paid for a certain number of years or until a certain age, such as 10 years or age 70. Then, depending on how you design the policy, you could either (a) stop the premiums at that point and then start to take the Social Security benefit to spend as part of your retirement income or (b) continue allocating a portion of your Social Security benefit to pay additional premiums on the life insurance policy and then spend the difference as you need or want.

This strategy provides a death benefit (which is the face amount of the life insurance policy, plus any increases to the face amount) to be paid out to your named beneficiaries, tax-free, when you pass away. This strategy can work in a number of ways. For example, it can be used to replenish the lost Social Security benefit at your death to provide for your spouse and/or children. Remember, once you pass away, your Social Security benefit stops. If you are married, your surviving spouse can collect your Social Security benefit, assuming your benefit is higher, but then his or her benefit will stop. That's because the surviving spouse only gets the higher of the two, not both. In addition, a long-term care rider can be added to the life insurance policy that can be used in the event you have to pay for long-term care expenses. You could also use this strategy to leave a financial legacy or to help replenish the value of your estate.

Strategy 10
Use Your IRA to Purchase a Cash Value Life Insurance Policy to Help Reduce Required Minimum Distributions (RMDs)

An often-used strategy is to take excess withdrawals, above your required cash flow needs, from your qualified retirement accounts or IRAs for the premiums on a cash value life insurance policy. The objective here is to spend down these retirement accounts in order to help minimize the amount of RMDs you must withdraw starting at age 70½. The after-tax withdrawals from your qualified retirement account or IRA are then used to pay the premiums on the cash value life insurance policy. This shifts dollars growing tax-deferred in the retirement accounts and subject to RMDs to the cash value of the life insurance policy where it can not only grow tax-deferred but can be accessed tax-free (via withdrawals up to the policy's cost basis and/or policy loans) and not be subject to RMDs. Remember, unlike the cash value and death benefit on a cash value life insurance policy, qualified retirement accounts and IRAs are only tax-deferred. With these retirement accounts, the tax *will be paid* at some point, whether it's by you or your beneficiaries. You can also utilize this same strategy with a Roth IRA conversion. Just keep in mind that whichever approach you use, it works best when you start early in retirement well before age 70½.

In addition, you can purchase a cash value life insurance policy to leave a tax-free death benefit (under current tax law) to your surviving spouse while your children inherit your qualified or tax-deferred retirement assets (e.g., IRAs).

Why would you do that? Because your surviving spouse won't have to deal with RMDs—required minimum distributions on qualified retirement accounts or IRAs—once he or she turns 70½. Instead, your spouse can take the tax-free death benefit and use it to generate retirement cash flow while your children take the RMDs from your IRA accounts. This is called a stretch IRA which is an estate-planning strategy that extends the tax-deferred status of an inherited IRA when it is passed on to a non-spouse beneficiary. The younger the beneficiary, the longer the tax-deferral (i.e., stretch) from the IRA. The term stretch IRA does not represent a specific type of IRA; rather it is a financial strategy that allows people to stretch out the life—and therefore the potential tax advantages—of an IRA. Keep in mind, you don't have to use your qualified retirement accounts or IRAs for this to work. You could pay the premiums on the life insurance policy using your Social Security benefit or any of your available liquid assets or cash flow from your nonretirement accounts as well.

Again, these are only some of many strategies you should consider. Your goal is to find the right strategy or strategies that work for you and for what you would like to accomplish.

Remember, when you retire it's all about maximizing cash flow and minimizing risk. This will allow you (and your spouse) to enjoy your retirement and not have to worry about whether or not your retirement income will last. Therefore, seek out the knowledge so you can understand how to make this happen. Thinking outside the box will help a great deal too.

Also, I can't emphasize enough the importance of seeking the advice and counseling of a true independent financial advisor, in particular, one who is obligated only to you and your best interests, not the financial firm they work for. This is why it's so important to work with an advisor who is not associated with Wall Street or one of the big brand-name or discount brokerage firms. Truly independent financial advisors are not subject to the sales quotas, conflicts of interest, or any of the other shenanigans that you get from those other firms. Plus, you are supporting small businesses, which are the backbone of our economy.

Finally, it's extremely important to make sure that the independent financial advisor you choose understands and embraces the importance of cash flow and guaranteed income.

----

[1] Qualified section 501(c) (3) charities and religious organizations generally don't pay income tax, therefore, that's not a concern if planning to leave money to them.

[2] http://www.moneychimp.com/features/market_cagr.htm

[3] This could incur a surrender penalty and/or a potential tax liability, so check

with your financial advisor or tax professional.

4 Consult the Social Security Administration website at SSA.gov to determine if the definition of "spouse" applies to your situation.

5 https://www.towerswatson.com/en/insights/newsletters/americas/insider/2012/annuities-and-retirement-happiness

CHAPTER 8

Recap and Final Thoughts

Let's take a moment to recap some of what you have learned, starting with a quick Q&A.

Q: Is a 401(k) a tax deduction or a tax deferral?
A: It's a tax deferral. Unlike a tax deduction, a tax deferral only reduces your taxes until some future date.

Q: You invest $100,000 and, after the first year, your rate of return is a positive 100 percent. Then, after the second year, your rate of return is a negative 50 percent. What is your average rate of return?
A: 25 percent (100 minus 50, divided by 2, equals 25).

Q: What is the value of the above investment account after the second year?
A: $100,000 (excluding applicable investment fees).

Q: What is the real or compounded rate of return of that investment after the second year?
A: Zero percent.

Q: During the accumulation phase, does it matter when the positive and negative rates of return take place?
A: No, as long as you don't do what many investors do—sell after the markets drop, then buy back in after they go back up.

Q: During the distribution phase, does it matter when the positive and negative rates of return take place?
A: Yes, it matters a great deal, especially if the returns are negative in the beginning. That's because it increases your risk of depleting your account, resulting in a loss of income or cash flow.

Q: Do as Wall Street __?, not as they__ ?
A: Do as Wall Street *does*, not as they *say*.

Q: What financial products can provide guaranteed lifetime income for you and your spouse, can potentially provide increasing income, and you can leave the account value to your beneficiaries?
A: Variable and fixed-index annuities with a guaranteed lifetime income benefit rider.

Q: Cash flow is _____?
A: King. I really hope this wasn't a difficult question! It wasn't without a lot of thought that I titled this book *Cash Flow Is King*. That's because we always have a need for cash flow. It's generally consistent and reliable especially compared to seeking a rate of return. Best of all, it can be guaranteed.

Recap of Chapters 1 through 7

In Chapter 1, I presented many financial misconceptions and how they can impact you and your money. As you should now see, much of what we have been taught simply isn't true. Everything is not always as it seems and in fact, it can often be misleading, especially, when it comes to the advice of Wall Street, the big brand-name and discount brokerage firms, and many of the media pundits. Remember, how you think is everything. It determines your behavior. You should now start to think differently. In addition, seek knowledge and not just information. It can be the difference between achieving financial success and security or not. Once you accept this, the rest will eventually take care of itself.

In Chapter 2, I explained sequence of investment returns risk and the impact market volatility can have on your investments. Market volatility can occur at any time and can adversely affect the value of your investments. Sequence of returns risk can potentially affect you in the early years of the retirement distribution phase if your returns are low or negative. In addition, I discussed asset correlation. Low correlation or noncorrelation are different from diversification. Both can potentially mitigate risk, but in different ways. A low- or noncorrelated investment strategy can potentially mitigate volatility risk, which diversification doesn't always do. Remember, your main objective should be to try to minimize losses. This is more important than trying to maximize gains. The math confirms this.

In Chapter 3, I explained the difference between how we have been taught to think about money compared with how the wealthy think about money. You should look to adopt the same philosophy about money as the wealthy do. As a guide, follow the seven steps that Warren Buffett used when he helped bail out Bank of America. For example, look to take calculated risks with your money and not risks based on hope, such as hoping the markets will go up. Be patient and think long term, as difficult as it may be at times. This may mean looking 10, 20, or more years out. Look for investment opportunities that come along periodically, because they eventually will. When they do, make sure you are prepared to take advantage of them by having funds that are available and accessible. Also, do as Wall Street *does*, not as they *say* by looking into how to utilize high cash value life insurance into your financial plan. I do and you should too. Remember, you certainly don't have to be wealthy to apply the principles and strategies that the wealthy use or saving and investing your money into many of the financial products they use.

In addition, don't be afraid to borrow or use leverage if it's beneficial from a financial and tax perspective. Consider the opportunity cost of your choices and decisions because it's a real cost to you. Like anything else, it's important to understand the pros and cons. Also, remember that liquidity is *not* an investor's or a retiree's friend. If you are investing for the long term, you certainly shouldn't be too concerned with it. If you need liquidity, even liquid at-risk investments are probably not where you should be putting your money in the first place.

Look to divide your assets among savings, liquid investments and illiquid investments based on your own personal situation. For example, consider dividing your assets into thirds: one-third in liquid no-risk assets, such as money markets or high cash value life insurance; one-third in liquid at-risk assets, such as stocks, bonds, mutual funds, and unit investment trusts; and one-third in illiquid at-risk assets that are not correlated to the markets, such as non-traded real estate investment trusts (non-traded REITs), private equity, or private loans.

At retirement, or leading up to retirement, you should incorporate annuities as well. Most annuities, such fixed and fixed-index annuities, generally fall into the category of illiquid no-risk assets. Variable annuities fall into this category when they have a guaranteed lifetime income benefit rider (the no-risk category is specifically due to the guaranteed lifetime income it provides, not on the account value). Although, some variable annuities can be structured to be liquid. Allocating your assets this way helps you cover all bases.

In Chapter 4, I used the analogy of a mountain climber whose initial goal is to reach the summit of the mountain. Many people may think that's the end goal; however, that is only half the goal. The other half of the goal is to get down from the summit safe and sound. Remember, the climber has only one shot at this. This also applies to the accumulation and distribution phases of retirement planning. You may have multiple attempts during the accumulation phase to get yourself to the point where you can retire comfortably or even retire at all. However, during the distribution phase, you probably won't be as fortunate. You most likely will have just one chance at getting it right.

Remember, too, that the financial and tax strategies used to get yourself *to* retirement are very different from those you should use *during* retirement. It's very important to understand the differences and utilize the appropriate savings, investments, financial products, and strategies, where applicable.

Chapter 5 starts to get into the heart and soul of the book—cash flow. That's because cash flow represents our financial lifeblood. You have likely heard the saying, "Let your money work for you, instead of you working for your money." When it comes to your savings and investments, that's what positive cash flow does—it works for you. Unfortunately, most of us have been taught to focus only on the rates of return we can get. This is not only an unreliable strategy, it can entail a lot of risk. Remember, there is nothing wrong with investing for growth. It should definitely be a part of your investment strategy, especially during the accumulation phase. It just shouldn't be your only strategy. However, cash flow should always be a part of your strategy, both in the accumulation phase—because it can be a big part of your rate of return and most certainly in the distribution phase—because it is what allows you to spend for both your needs and your wants during retirement.

I also shared a number of savings, investments, and financial products to which you can consider allocating your funds to generate cash flow. Some of them have little to no risk to your principal, while others incur risk to your principal. Certain ones can be used during both the accumulation and distribution phases (such as mutual funds, real estate, or private equity). Annuities can technically be used in either phase too—but it is generally best to use them as you approach retirement and definitely during retirement.

Chapter 6 is all about how to not outlive your retirement income by creating your own personalized private pension plan. People love pensions and Social Security. That's understandable, because they provide reliable cash flow every month. As a result, you don't have to worry about stock market losses or crashes, the negative impact of interest rates changes, or a weak economic environment (i.e., a recession).

However, many people also like to keep some level of control and flexibility—and it's certainly smart to, when possible. That's why a variable or fixed-index annuity with a guaranteed lifetime income benefit rider is so important to understand and consider in your retirement plan. Remember, these annuities are not investments. They are financial products that provide guaranteed lifetime income, like a pension. Therefore, be sure to view them as such. However, unlike a pension, they can provide the potential to access the account value if needed or wanted and you can leave any remaining account value to your beneficiaries. This is exactly what most people want. Unfortunately, much of what people may hear regarding annuities may be negative. Again, because of the lack of knowledge and misleading and self-serving information people have been exposed to. Therefore, you shouldn't believe everything you read or hear, especially when it comes from your friends, family, the internet, media pundits, Wall Street, or the big brand-name and discount brokerage firms. Don't allow false or inaccurate information to deter you from making an appropriate decision that's right for you and your family.

Also, be especially wary of opinions that are never substantiated. There are plenty of independent and unbiased sources to help you substantiate the benefits and value of using an annuity with a guaranteed lifetime income benefit rider based on math and facts. Feel free to contact me and I will be happy to forward to you this information.

Chapter 7 is about creating your ideal retirement plan. Remember, in retirement you will no longer receive a paycheck from your employer or business. Instead, you will start to receive your income from Social Security, perhaps a pension, what you have saved and invested, or some combination of these. Since you can't live off rates of return, you need to create a cash flow strategy, ideally, one that can maximize your cash flow with the least amount of risk possible.

I also explained where you should start when creating your ideal retirement plan. The place to start is at the end, then work your way back. I also provided strategies for the retirement distribution phase to help get you thinking about the different ways to structure your plan for generating cash flow during retirement and structure it so you don't run out. Your plan should cover your essential needs, but also provide for your wants. To help you accomplish this, I recommend working with an independent financial advisor, in particular, an advisor who is obligated to work in your best interest (fiduciary responsibility) and not the firm he or she works for. Equally important, find an advisor who is not caught up in chasing performance or rates of return, but instead one who embraces the philosophy of cash flow, particularly guaranteed cash flow. He or she can help you create a plan and provide appropriate strategies that will work specifically for you and your family.

I also discussed how retirees will face new risks during the distribution phase, risks that are not of concern during the accumulation phase. One of these is longevity risk—the risk that you will outlive your retirement assets and the income they generate. This is often said to be the new retirement risk as a result of people living longer and, in some cases, retiring sooner. In addition to longevity risk, there is inflation risk, market risk, volatility risk, and sequence of returns risk. Plus, there are healthcare and potential long-term care expenses that are valid concerns and present additional risk to retirees.

Fortunately, with the proper planning and advice, you can likely mitigate and even outsource these risks. You may not be able to outsource all the risks or every risk, but something is certainly better than nothing. These risks and potential unknown expenses always carry the possibility of becoming a huge financial burden for retirees. Therefore, be sure to obtain the proper types of insurance policies and the adequate amount of coverage from these policies.

Final Thoughts

The truth can't be denied forever. Therefore, I hope you not only see the truths but the value and benefits of the principles and strategies I've shared. Look to apply them for yourself and your family. There really is no reason not to. I have provided data and examples, confirmed by the math and independent research. And now that you understand what is going on and have this knowledge, you should know what to do and can take the appropriate actions. As I mentioned in the beginning, I personally use the principles and strategies in this book as well. I have the benefit of many years of real-world experience and also practice what I preach.

On your journey for financial knowledge, beware of the naysayers. They are out there and will try to discredit the facts and the math of what has been presented to you, not just in this book, but also regarding the independent research that's been conducted by the PhDs in the field of finance and economics. Believe me, I see this happening all the time. The naysayers will give plenty of reasons (actually… they are just excuses) that they freely share as to why you shouldn't do something. However, their opinions are just that—opinions. Yet, there is nothing that actually supports their opinions. The math doesn't and the facts don't. They also, for the most part, have bought into the misconceptions discussed in Chapter 1. They simply refuse to be open-minded and certainly don't think outside the box. And just as important, they simply can't speak for or understand each and every person's objectives, concerns, and risk tolerance. Keep in mind, the very reason they think the way they do is that they are getting their information from the very same self-serving sources I have mentioned throughout this book. This is why it's so important to stay focused on the math and the facts. Don't allow the false and inaccurate information from these naysayers sway you from doing what you believe is right for you and your family. Remember, if they do convince you and your plan fails, they certainly won't be around to bail you out.

This is also why you should avoid seeking out the opinion of your friends, family, coworkers, accountant, etc. They are not experts in this area, nor do they have the proper training or knowledge to give you the right or appropriate advice when it comes to saving, investing, and financial planning. Reading magazines on personal finance, taking investment classes at the local college, or even having "lots of money" doesn't qualify them either. Just like the naysayers, they are most likely getting their information from all the flawed sources I've mentioned. Remember, good intentions do not equate to good advice, and certainly not advice that is most appropriate for you. Therefore, do what's best for you so that you can feel comfortable about *your own* situation. It always helps to keep an open-mind and, of course, to think outside the box.

Don't be pennywise and dollar foolish either. Yes, fees do matter, but not more than understanding what you are getting for the fees you are paying; it's about the value and benefits you receive for those fees. If you are paying more for something, yet it is providing you with something of value that's beneficial to you or your family, then the extra fee is very likely worth it. Again, the independent research confirms this. Remember, there is no free lunch.

The good news is, because of your newfound knowledge, you are now much better prepared to question, or better yet, ignore what Wall Street, the big brand-name and discount brokerage firms, most of the media pundits, and the naysayers tell you to do with your money. You can now pursue more appropriate advice for managing your money by working with an independent financial advisor and learning from those who have actually done independent and unbiased research regarding wealth management and retirement planning. In particular, I highly recommend the work of Dr. Moshe Milevsky and Tom Hegna. In addition, there are plenty of very good financial books (I have provided recommendations at the end of this book) and white papers available that are based on the math and facts.

Be sure to share this book with the people you care about such as your children, grandchildren, and other family and friends to learn these concepts and strategies. This can help teach them to think outside the financial box and like the wealthy which can then help guide them down the right path and not be influenced by misleading and self-serving sources or fall into the traps of the misconceptions I've discussed. The earlier they start, the better off and easier it will be for them later.

Remember that you sacrificed (or will sacrifice) to save and invest for your future goals, whether it's for your children's college education, a second home, or your retirement. You may have sacrificed a little or perhaps a lot, but you did (or will) sacrifice by putting your hard-earned money into IRAs, a 401(k), or other types of savings and investment accounts. As a result, that money couldn't be used for other things you may have wanted or needed at the time. Therefore, why sacrifice during your retirement if you don't need to? You should be enjoying your retirement and doing the things that you would like to do. To accomplish this, your primary objective should be to structure your retirement assets to generate maximum cash flow on a reliable and even guaranteed basis while also minimizing the risks.

If you could structure your retirement distribution phase so that you didn't have to worry about the direction of the stock market, interest rates, or the state of the economy, why wouldn't you? Do you really want to spend your time in retirement watching over all of this or having to worry about it? If you could simply receive a check each and every month that would pay your bills, cover unexpected needs, and allow you to do all the other things that make life fun and worthwhile, wouldn't you want that?

Remember, it's not about which retirement plan may be the most successful—this can only be determined with 20-20 hindsight. Instead, it should be about which retirement plan offers the *least chance* to fail you. Therefore, if you want guarantees, then seek guarantees. If you want less risk, then seek less risk. If you want independent personalized financial advice and planning, then seek independent personalized financial advice and planning.

Most important, always think in terms of cash flow, because cash flow allows you to continue to pay for the things you need and the things you want throughout your life. Cash flow also allows you to save and invest toward your future goals, which of course, include retirement. In fact, keep in mind that the whole purpose of saving and investing for retirement is to eventually create cash flow from the savings and investments so you can spend it on the things you need and want.

If you are in the accumulation phase, think of which cash flow strategies you can use to help maximize the growth of your assets. If you are in the distribution phase, think of which cash flow strategies you can use to help maximize your retirement income with the least amount of risk. In the end, that's truly the goal. Rates of return can't do that. However, cash flow can, and that's why **cash flow is king**!

I am here to help. I can personally work with you or recommend an independent financial advisor who understands and embraces the principles and strategies in this book. Feel free to contact me for more information. I would love to assist any way I can.

Please contact me at:

mark@mappawm.com

or

visit my website at:

www.mappawm.com

Book Recommendations

I love to learn as well as educate others about financial planning and money management. I read a lot of books on these topics, and as a result, I am always learning new ideas and gaining more knowledge. I highly encourage you to do the same. Below are my book recommendations to reinforce what I have shared with you. They will further assist you with your ongoing pursuit of financial knowledge and help you to think differently. You will then be much better prepared to make the most appropriate financial decisions for you and your family. Enjoy!

Pay Checks and Play Checks by Tom Hegna

The Retirement Savings Time Bomb... and How to Defuse It by Ed Slott

Pensionize Your Nest Egg: How to Use Product Allocation to Create a Guaranteed Income For Life by Moshe A. Milevsky, PhD and Alexandra C. Macqueen, CFP

Confessions of a CPA by Bryan S. Bloom

Becoming Your Own Banker by R. Nelson Nash

The Case for IBC: How To Secede From Our Current Monetary Regime One Household At A Time by R. Nelson Nash, L. Carlos Lara, and Robert P. Murphy

The Wealth Code by Jason Vanclef

Discovering Hidden Treasures by Dan Thompson

Money. Wealth. Life Insurance. by Jake Thompson

The Bankers Code by George Antone

Pirates of Manhattan by Barry James Dyke

Pirates of Manhattan II: Highway to Serfdom by Barry James Dyke

A Path to Financial Peace of Mind by Dwayne Burnell, MBA

The Power of Zero: How to Get to the 0% Tax Bracket and Transform Your Retirement by David McKnight

Retirement Heist: How Companies Plunder and Profit from the Nest Eggs of American Workers by Ellen E. Schultz

Creature from Jekyll Island: A Second Look at the Federal Reserve by G. Edward Griffin

Bailout: An Inside Account of How Washington Abandoned Main Street While Rescuing Wall Street by Neil Barofsky

Wall Street, Banks, and American Foreign Policy by Murray N. Rothbard

The Great Wall Street Retirement Scam by Rick Bueter

Several of these authors have multiple books published that I did not list above. I highly suggest you read them as well.

Acknowledgments

There are many people I wish to acknowledge and thank who have helped shape my career as a financial advisor or helped me during the process of writing this book. In particular, I would like to thank the following people. I would like to thank R. Nelson Nash who, years ago, taught me the value in creating my own cash flow system that I control and how to go about it so my family and I can rely solely on ourselves and not on outside financial institutions. Much of how I think about money and cash flow is from what I have learned from Nelson. I would like to thank Zack Mappa, Marilyn Ferdinand, Dave Wankowski, Julie Wankowski, and Sara Tumpane for taking the time to read the drafts of my book and providing candid feedback and suggestions. I would like to thank Tanya Widner for her reviews and feedback of the drafts as well and for everything she does in running the daily operations of Mappa Wealth Management. I would like to thank Brook Ford for her dedication and support that she brings to Mappa Wealth Management. I would like to thank Susan Zangler for helping me to get this book off and running and providing helpful and candid suggestions and ideas. I would like to thank Barry Levy for his brilliant coaching and marketing support that have helped with the growth of Mappa Wealth Management. Finally, I would like to thank Steve Wilhusen and Brett Gardiner for being great colleagues at Mappa Wealth Management. We all share the same vision of doing what is best for our clients and I look forward to working with you as we continue that journey.

About the Author

Mark Mappa is the founder, president, and managing principal at Mappa Wealth Management. He has over 30 years of experience in financial planning and wealth management.

As a fiduciary and independent financial advisor, Mark provides objective advice that is tailored to meet each client's specific and individual situation and that is designed to help them reach their stated financial goals. He does this by taking the time to listen to his clients and to truly understand their goals and objectives. He also prides himself on being able to explain difficult financial topics in a way that is easily understood.

Mark's years of experience as an independent financial advisor has led to a philosophy and perspective about financial planning that he incorporates into the strategies he develops for each of his clients. While everyone's strategy is unique to them, Mark believes that the underlying philosophy of a successful financial plan includes: thinking in terms of cash flow, investing like the wealthy, protecting the downside of your investments, and thinking outside the financial box.

Mark has written numerous financial articles and has appeared on the television show *The Stock Market Observer*. Mark is also an authorized infinite banking concept (IBC) practitioner through the Nelson Nash Institute.

Mark holds the following financial industry credentials:

- Master of Science in Financial Services (MSFS)
- Certified Financial Planner Practitioner™ (CFP®)
- Chartered Financial Consultant (ChFC)
- Chartered Life Underwriter (CLU)
- Registered Financial Consultant (RFC)
- Certified Fund Specialist (CFS)
- Certified Income Specialist (CIS)
- Certified Estate and Trust Specialist (CES)

Mark and his wife, Rachel, have been married for more than 23 years. They have three children—Zackary, Tanner, and Sophie—all of whom Mark has coached in the various sports they have played over the years. Mark loves to read books on financial and economic topics. He is also a Corvette enthusiast and enjoys concerts, sports, vacationing, and spending time at the family's Florida home.

About Mappa Wealth Management

It's about partnership.

Mappa Wealth Management is your long-term partner for navigating financial and life decisions. We help you achieve the best life possible and work with you to make this happen. We bring clarity to complex financial concepts by taking time to explain our approach and making sure you're actively involved in cultivating your personalized financial plan. Working with you in anticipation of life's transitions, we can help make sure you're financially prepared for challenges ahead.

Committed to integrity and transparency, as fiduciaries we take pride in upholding the highest ethical standards. Our clients' best interests are always our number one concern. We're here when you need us, in good times and bad. Acting as your voice of reason, we can help assess important life decisions by offering an objective, well-researched and competent opinion. We're devoted to your financial well-being.

With passion and dedication, Mappa Wealth Management strives to positively impact the lives of our clients every day. For us, it's always about partnership.

Clients who partner with Mappa Wealth Management receive:

- Unbiased and objective advice from independent financial advisors.
- Personalized financial and investment advice. No "one-size-fits-all" strategy or plan.
- Decades of knowledge and experience. We have seen the good times and the challenging times and we can help you navigate through both.
- Recommendations and support from an independent and privately-owned firm. We are not bound by sales quotas or proprietary products.

Mappa Wealth Management is a comprehensive Wealth Management firm headquartered in the north suburbs of Chicago, Illinois with other locations throughout the area. Mappa Wealth Management adheres to fiduciary standards and, as such, provides financial planning, retirement planning, investment and money management, estate planning, insurance and risk management, retirement income distribution planning, business financial consulting, employee financial wellness workshops, and 401(k) review and management. Mappa Wealth Management also has a long-standing partnership with Quorum Federal Credit Union,[1] offering wealth management and financial planning services to their members, including employees of Kraft Heinz (formerly Kraft Foods) and Mondelez International.

———

[1] NOT FDIC, NCUA/NCUSIF INSURED | NOT A DEPOSIT | NOT GUARANTEED BY ANY BANK OR CREDIT UNION | NOT INSURED BY ANY FEDERAL GOVERNMENT AGENCY | FUNDS MAY LOSE VALUE | NOT A CONDITION OF ANY BANKING OR CREDIT UNION ACTIVITY

Made in the USA
Columbia, SC
22 February 2020